Side Hustle Kickstart: A Side hustle planner with 90 Days to Start Earning with a Simple Plan

Evan West

Contents

Part 4
Your Momentum Toolkit

Welcome & How to Use This Planner

You're here because you want more than a pay check. You want the freedom to earn extra money on your own terms, using skills you already have or are willing to learn. The fact that you picked up this planner means you're ready to take action, and the next 90 days will help you do exactly that.

A side hustle is not about working nonstop or creating a second full-time job. It's about building a small income stream that fits your life. You don't need a business degree, big startup money, or a huge audience. You just need the willingness to test ideas, take small steps, and learn as you go.

This planner guides you through a simple roadmap to launch a profitable side hustle in three months. Every page is designed to help you make decisions, try real-world strategies, and get paid for something you can offer. You'll be building one step at a time: researching, validating, creating, and selling - without pressure, confusion, or guesswork.

Use this as your daily coach. Show up, do the small tasks, and let consistency work for you. If you follow this layout, your efforts compound into progress, then into profit.

How to Use This Planner

This is not a blank notebook. It's a guided system with daily and weekly actions designed to help you build, launch, and improve a side hustle step by step. Here's how to use it effectively:

Follow the 90-Day Roadmap

This planner is divided into three phases:

Weeks 1–4: Choose & Validate

You'll test ideas, research customers, and confirm what people actually want.

Weeks 5–8: Build & Launch

You'll create an offer, set pricing, develop a simple marketing presence, and start selling.

Weeks 9–12: Sell & Scale

You'll improve your product, increase visibility, and create consistent income habits.

You do not skip ahead. You complete each phase before moving on.

Show Up Daily (Even on Busy Days)

Each day, you'll complete:

One **Quick Win**, a **Core Priority** and one **Connection Task**

These actions work together to make progress and attract paying customers. Even 30 minutes counts.

Use the Weekly Checklists and Reviews

At the start of each week, you'll set goals with focus and clarity. At the end, you'll review what worked, what didn't, and what to adjust. Your goal isn't perfection - it's learning through action.

Your reviews will become your biggest source of improvement and profit.

Treat This Like a Small Experiment

You're testing ideas, not carving them in stone. If something isn't working, you won't force it - you'll pivot using the feedback you collect. This mindset saves time, money, and energy.

Track Money from Day One

You'll track:

• Daily time spent

• Daily and weekly income

• Costs and expenses

• Customer responses and results

Even small wins matter. Seeing real numbers helps you stay motivated and see growth clearly.

Celebrate Milestones

This planner includes checkpoints to celebrate:

First sale

First customer review

First repeat sale

Profit on a product or service

Weekly or monthly income goals

Reward progress. Small wins lead to income you can build on.

Your Commitment

You don't need to work harder. You simply need to take consistent, intentional action. Small steps become skills. Skills become income. Income becomes freedom.

Turn the page when you're ready to begin. Your 90-day journey starts now.

Part 1
Prepare to Launch

Chapter 1
What a Side Hustle
Really Is (and Isn't)

Before you start building your income stream, it helps to understand what a side hustle actually means. Many people imagine it has to be a huge idea, a perfect brand, or a big investment. The truth is much simpler.

A side hustle is a small, flexible way to earn extra money without quitting your job or rearranging your life. It helps you turn skills you already have into something valuable for real people. You don't need to wait for the "right moment." You start small, learn as you go, and improve through experience.

✓ What a Side Hustle IS

A side hustle is a practical business experiment.

You try something useful, offer it to real people, and see what works.

A side hustle starts with helping someone solve a simple problem. It might save them time, reduce stress, fix something, teach them a skill, or make life easier. You don't need a brand-new idea — you only need a helpful one.

A side hustle grows through small, consistent actions. You don't spend months preparing or perfecting a website before you have anything to sell. You test quickly, make real-world improvements, and upgrade only when income begins to come in.

Above all, a side hustle **fits the life you already have.** You build it around your schedule, not the other way around. Even ten minutes a day can move you forward if you focus on the right things.

> A true side hustle is low risk, useful to someone, and built step by step through action, not perfection

✗ What a Side Hustle ISN'T

A side hustle is **not**:

- a second full-time job

- something that needs a huge audience

- a passion project with no paying customers

- a get-rich-fast strategy

- a copy of someone else's business model

You don't need to "hustle harder." You don't need to work nights and weekends until you collapse. You don't need to spend months preparing before you ever make an offer. The fastest path to income is testing a simple idea quickly, not building a complicated one slowly.

Your side hustle should **bring possibility into your life not pressure.**

Why This Matters

When you know what a side hustle truly is, you can stop trying to be perfect. You can stop overthinking, overplanning, and comparing yourself to businesses that took years to grow. You can start small, learn fast, and create something that works.

This planner will guide you through that process so you can build something real, one step at a time. Not someday. Not when you feel "ready." Now.

The goal isn't to hustle harder. the goal is to earn smarter

Turn the page to begin the simple 90-day method that will take you from idea to income.

Chapter 2
The 90-Day Method

Launching a side hustle doesn't happen by accident. It happens through small, targeted actions that build on each other. This planner uses a simple three-phase approach that helps you go from idea to income in just 90 days, without overwhelm and without wasting your time on things that don't matter.

Each phase has one goal, one priority, and one set of small, repeatable tasks. You don't need to do everything. You just need to do the right things at the right time.

Phase 1: Choose & Validate (Weeks 1–4)

> ## Goal: Pick ONE profitable idea and confirm that people want it.

Before you make anything, you must confirm that your idea has potential. The next four weeks are about testing, not building. Your job is to choose an idea that solves a real problem, that real people are willing to pay to fix.

You're not here to guess. You're here to gather proof.

Why Phase 1 Matters

Too many people start with logos, websites, branding, and then spend months building something that no one ends up buying. This planner helps you avoid wasted time and wasted effort by focusing on the only thing that matters first:

Does someone want this enough to pay for it?

If you can prove the answer is yes, you're ready to build. If not, you adjust before you waste time and energy.

What You'll Do in This Phase

1. Brainstorm and Compare Possible Ideas

You'll list your skills, interests, and practical offers you could provide. Then you will compare them based on:

• Demand (Do people need this?)

- Value (Does it solve a problem?)

- Time (Can you deliver this with your schedule?)

- Profit (Can it earn without costing too much to create?)

This step helps you avoid ideas that sound exciting but won't pay you.

2. Identify Who Your Customer Would Be

You don't need a huge audience — you just need a small group of people with a shared need. You'll define:

Who they are, what problem they have, and why they would pay for a solution.

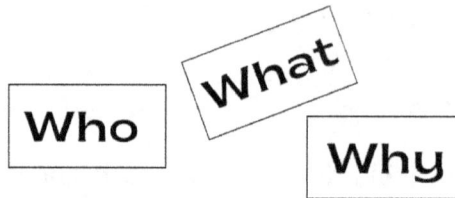

Clarity here makes selling easier later.

3. Ask Real People What They Need

You'll collect feedback from real people using short, simple questions. You're not asking if they "like" your idea. You're asking:

Do they struggle with this?

Are they looking for help?

Have they paid for similar solutions before?

What result do they want?

You'll be learning from potential customers — not guessing.

. . .

4. Validate Through Interest and Feedback

Interest is not measured by compliments. It is measured by action. You're looking for signs like:

People asking when it will be ready, people telling you they wish they had it sooner or people wanting more information.

Words are nice. Action is validation.

5. Conduct Simple Pricing Checks

Instead of asking "What should I charge?" you'll ask:

"What have you paid for this before?"

"What would be fair for this result?"

"Would you pay more for faster results or a higher-quality version?"

You don't need exact pricing yet, you need a confident range.

6. Decide Which Idea to Move Forward With

After gathering everything, you'll choose one validated idea using the decision worksheet. The goal isn't perfection. The goal is choosing the idea with the best earning potential and the strongest problem-solving value.

What You Will NOT Do Yet

During Weeks 1–4, you do **not**:

build a website,

design branding,

create logos or packaging,

spend money on tools or ads,

OR make a perfect version of anything

Those things are distractions at this stage. They come later, when you already know you have something people want.

In Phase 1, your idea must earn interest before it ever earns income.

Tools You'll Use in This Phase

Throughout these four weeks, you'll be using:

• **Skills & Passion Worksheet** — to generate strong business ideas

• **Customer Mini-Survey & Feedback Prompts** — to gather real data

• **Validation Checklist** — to confirm which ideas have potential

• **Pricing Feedback Tracker** — to estimate what customers will pay

• **Decision Page: "Choose Your Idea"** — to commit to one offer

These tools help remove guesswork, pressure, and confusion.

End-of-Phase Outcome

At the end of Week 4, you will have:

- ONE validated idea you feel confident about
- A specific customer profile and problem you are solving
- A starting price range based on real feedback
- A clear direction for Phase 2 so you know exactly what to build next

Your idea is chosen. Your customers are real. Your price is grounded in truth, not fear. Now you're ready to create something people will pay for.

Turn the page and let's start gathering your strengths and possibilities.

Phase 2: Build & Launch (Weeks 5–8)

> # Goal: Create a simple offer and start selling it.

Now that you've validated your idea, it's time to build the first version of your product or service and launch it — not perfectly, but practically. You're moving from ideas and research into real-world action. The goal is not to build the best version. The goal is to create the *simplest version that people can buy right now.*

This is where your side hustle becomes real.

Why Phase 2 Matters

Most beginners wait too long to sell. They build secretly behind the scenes, spend money too early, try to make everything perfect, and launch months after they had their first spark. Meanwhile, someone with a simpler idea launches first and gets customers.

Success comes from speed of learning, not perfection of planning.

You learn more from one paying customer than from fifty hours of thinking.

Your first version teaches you what your audience actually wants. Once you have feedback, and money coming in, you can improve with confidence.

What You'll Do in This Phase

1. Build a Minimum Viable Product or Service (MVP)

Your MVP is the most basic version of your product or service that still delivers value. This version: solves the core problem, does NOT try to be perfect, and takes the least time and money to create

Examples:

• A coach offering a 2-session starter package

• A designer offering a simple logo + social media icon bundle

• A baker selling a small test batch of 12 themed cupcakes

• A crafter selling a limited run product to gauge demand

• A marketer offering a one-off audit instead of long contracts

The key is to **start small, deliver value, and improve later.**

2. Create a Simple Offer Page, Post, or PDF

You don't need a full website. You need **a clear offer and a clear way to pay.** Your offer can live on:

a social media post

a single link page (Linktree, PayPal, Gumroad, etc.)

a one-page document or PDF flyer sent by message

a basic landing page built in minutes

Your offer needs:

- what you provide

- who it's for

- what problem it solves

- what the result or benefit is

- how much it costs

- how they can buy it

Clarity sells. Complexity stalls.

3. Write Your First Sales Message

You'll write a simple message or post that:

• names the problem

• presents your offer

• shares the benefit

• shows the price

• gives a clear call to action (example: DM to book, click to buy, order here)

Customers don't need hype. They need help.

4. Collect Payment in Easy Ways

Forget complicated payment systems and advanced setups. Choose the simplest way people can pay you right now, such as:

PayPal

Cash App

Stripe link

Etsy listing

Buy Me a Coffee

Sellfy or Gumroad for digital goods

In-person payment for physical products

If someone wants to pay, **don't make it hard.**

. . .

5. Gather Customer Feedback Immediately

Once your first customers experience your offer, you'll ask:

• What did you like most?

• What could be better?

• Would you recommend this to someone else?

• What would you pay for an improved version?

Feedback is gold. It tells you what to adjust before you scale.

Feedback replaces guessing. Sales replace fear.

What You Will NOT Do Yet

During Weeks 5–8, you do **not**:

aim for perfection

spend weeks on a fancy website

wait for "more followers"

lower prices out of fear

build the big version before the small one

Your first version doesn't need to be perfect. It only needs to exist.

Tools You'll Use in This Phase

You'll use:

• **Offer Builder Worksheet** – to define your product/service clearly

• **MVP Checklist** – to build the simplest version that sells

• **Simple Sales Message Template** – to promote your offer

• **Pricing & Profit Worksheet** – to choose a price that works

• **Customer Feedback Tracker** – to improve your product

These tools guide you step by step so you launch confidently and quickly.

End-of-Phase Outcome

By the end of Week 8, you will have:

- An offer that can earn income
- A simple payment method ready to use
- A launch message you can share multiple times
- A business that is open for real customers

Your idea is no longer just an idea. People can buy it. You are officially a business owner.

Turn the page to learn how to sell and scale smarter, not harder.

Phase 3: Sell & Scale (Weeks 9–12)

> # Goal: Improve the offer, increase visibility, and create consistent income habits.

You now have a real offer and real customers. These last four weeks are about selling smarter, not working harder. You're no longer guessing what people might want. You have proof, feedback, and income — even if small. Phase 3 builds on that by improving your offer and creating simple systems that make selling easier and more consistent.

You are moving from "trying something" to "growing something."

Why Phase 3 Matters

Most new business owners skip improvement and jump straight into expansion. They add more products, try to scale too fast, and exhaust their time and resources. But the most profitable businesses don't grow wide - they grow *deep*. They improve one offer until it becomes efficient, profitable, and desirable.

Customers teach you how to grow. Data replaces guesswork.

Your goal now is to listen to customers, respond to their needs, and become better at serving one market with one great solution.

What You'll Do in This Phase

1. Promote Your Offer More Frequently and Strategically

You will share your offer more often without "selling harder." Instead, you will:

• Share testimonials and feedback

• Highlight results or benefits

• Explain who the offer is perfect for

• Show before/after possibilities

• Post short stories or examples of value

Visibility increases trust. Trust increases sales.

2. Improve Your Product/Service Using Customer Feedback

You'll review feedback gathered from Phase 2:

What did customers love?

What confused them?

What did they wish existed?

What could be faster, clearer, simpler?

Improvement doesn't mean making it bigger. It means making it better.

Examples:

• A coaching package might add worksheets for clarity

• A physical product might improve durability or packaging

• A digital product might add a step-by-step guide

• A service might include a faster delivery option

Little upgrades create big value.

• • •

3. Raise or Adjust Pricing if Needed

If customers are happy, returning, or referring others, that's data. If your time investment is too large for the price you charge, that's data too.

You may:

Increase price

Add a premium option

Create a smaller or starter version for beginners

Offer bulk or bundle pricing

The right price honors your value and your time.

4. Add One Repeatable Marketing Habit

You will commit to one consistent action that supports sales. Choose a habit you can maintain weekly, such as:

Posting value content on social media

Sending one weekly email

Sharing a customer story or result

DM outreach to potential leads

Local promotion (flyers, community groups, word-of-mouth)

You don't need more strategies. You need one you repeat.

Consistency builds pipelines. Pipelines generate predictable income.

5. Track Income, Time, Profit, and Conversion

You'll collect simple business data:

How much money came in?

How much time did it require?

Which actions led to sales?

What percentage of inquiries became customers?

This data helps you:

- Raise prices with confidence

- Stop doing things that don't work

- Double down on what does

Tracking teaches you how to earn smarter.

6. Build Simple Processes to Save Time

You will create small systems such as: Pre-written responses to common questions, templates for promotions or order messages, a repeatable delivery process, and automated or easy payment links.

Systems reduce stress. They make earning repeatable, not random.

What You Will NOT Do

During Weeks 9–12, you will NOT:

try to scale without improvement

add a second idea before the first is earning

ignore what paying customers want

expand too quickly

work harder without working smarter

Success comes from refining one offer - not building ten.

Tools You'll Use in This Phase

• **Sales Message Variations** - for repeated promotion without sounding repetitive

• **Test & Improve Worksheet** - to turn feedback into upgrades

• **Weekly Marketing Habit Builder** - to establish consistent visibility

• **Income + Expense Tracking Pages** - to track profit and pricing decisions

• **Customer Testimonial Capture Pages** - to gather social proof that sells for you

These tools help remove fear, replace guessing with data, and build confidence in your offer.

End-of-Phase Outcome

By the end of Week 12, you will:

- Earn money based on a real offer
- Know what truly improves sales
- Have a reliable marketing habit
- Continue or expand with confidence

Your business becomes predictable instead of accidental. You know what works, what to change, and how to sell consistently.

Chapter 3
Identify Your Strengths

Skills, passions, market value prompts

Skills, passions, and market value prompts

Before you choose your best side hustle idea, you need to understand what you already bring to the marketplace. Strong businesses are built on value that comes naturally to you, paired with something people need. Your most profitable idea often lives where three things overlap:

What you can do

What you enjoy

What people are willing to pay for

The next pages help you find that overlap clearly, without guessing.

A) Your Skills

Skills are things you can do well enough that someone would want your help with them. They might come from your job, hobbies, personal experience, or things you have learned over time.

Think about the abilities you use without noticing how valuable they are. Many of the skills that feel easy to you are difficult for someone else.

Types of Skills You Might Have

• Technical skills such as editing, baking, coding, photography, bookkeeping, or hair styling

• Creative skills such as writing, crafting, designing, video editing, or drawing

• Service skills such as teaching, organizing, planning, tutoring, or customer support

• Problem solving skills such as research, budgeting, repairing, simplifying tasks, or finding useful information

• People skills such as guiding, mentoring, communicating, negotiating, or teaching

Skill Prompts

Use these questions to uncover your strongest skills:

What do people usually ask you for help with

What tasks do you do quickly or easily compared to others

What skills have you built through work, hobbies, or life experience

What skills have you shown in unpaid settings such as helping friends or family?

Worksheet: Top Skills

Take your time. Honest answers here will lead to profitable choices later.

Worksheet: Top Skills

Skill	How I learned it	What problem it solves	Will someone pay for this (y / n)

B) Your Passions

Passions are things you look forward to doing. They bring you satisfaction and you feel proud when they are done well.Not every passion should become a business, but the right ones can give you energy to grow your income.

Passion Prompts

Write down:

- What activities feel rewarding or satisfying

- What topics you can talk about for hours

- What you enjoy doing even when it requires effort

- What you would keep doing even without praise or attention

Worksheet: What Energizes You

Passion supports consistency. Consistency creates income.

Worksheet: What Energizes You

Activity	Why I enjoy it	Who benefits from it	Possible offer idea

C) Market Value

Market value means people are willing to pay for a solution. A skill or passion becomes a side hustle only when it solves a problem clearly enough that someone would purchase the result.

Your goal is to match your abilities with needs that already exist.

Market Value Prompts

Answer clearly:

What problem does my skill or passion help someone solve?

Who needs help with this problem?

What result does this person get when they receive my help?

Have people paid for similar solutions or services before?

Do people search online or ask for help with this problem?

Market Demand Check

Answer clearly:

Market Demand Check

Question	Yes	No
Are people currently paying for similar solutions	☐	☐
Can I deliver a version of this without delay	☐	☐
Is the problem urgent or annoying for customers	☐	☐
Does solving it save someone time, stress, or money	☐	☐
Do people already ask for help solving it	☐	☐

If most answers are yes, you have something valuable.

If most answers are yes, you have something valuable.

D) Your Strength Overlap

Once you complete the skill, passion, and market value prompts, you can find your strongest income potential.

Find Your Intersection

Fill in each line: one skill I have, one passion I want to keep using:, one problem I can solve for others? Then answer: what can I offer that solves this problem, how can I deliver it in a simple way to start, who will get the most benefit from it?

Worksheet: Strength to Offer Brainstorm

Skill	Passion	Problem I can solve	Possible offer

Review your answers. You are forming a business idea based on what you do naturally and what people already need.

E) Reflection Prompts

Take a moment to reflect. Write a few sentences for each:

Which strengths stood out the most

_____

_____

Which skills or passions could help someone quickly

_____

_____

Which problems do people often bring to me

_____

_____

Who seems to need my help the most

_____

_____

Which idea excites me and also seems profitable

_____

_____

Decision Highlight

Circle or mark ideas that match all three:

✓ I have the skill

✓ I enjoy the work

✓ People would pay to solve this problem

Ideas that meet all three criteria are the best ones to explore during validation.

Chapter 4
Quick Idea Generator Page
Prompts + mini worksheet

Your strengths can become income when they solve a real problem for someone else. This page helps you turn your skills and passions into simple side hustle ideas without overthinking. You are not choosing your final idea here. You are only generating possibilities to test later.

> Focus on ideas that are simple, useful, and realistic to deliver.

A) Idea Prompts

Answer the following questions with short, specific responses. Write the first things that come to mind. Your ideas do not need to be perfect or unique at this stage.

Prompts

- Who needs help solving a problem I can fix quickly

- What skill can I offer as a small service or product

- What result can I help someone achieve more easily

- What do people already ask me to do or teach

- How could I help someone save time, reduce stress, or reach a goal

- What solution could I create in less than two weeks

Write freely. Even tiny ideas can become profitable when tested properly.

B) Mini Worksheet: Turn a Strength Into an Idea

Use this four step exercise to convert any strength into a practical offer someone might buy.

Step 1: Choose a Skill or Passion

Write one skill or activity you are capable of doing well.

Step 2: Define the Problem It Solves

What difficulty, challenge, or need does this help someone overcome

Step 3: Describe the Result Someone Gets

What positive outcome would a person receive by buying your solution

Step 4: Create a Simple Offer Idea

Think of something you can teach, make, fix, plan, organize, design, deliver, cook, or complete.

My skill or passion:

_____

_____

The problem it solves:

_____

_____

The result someone gets:

_____

_____

Possible offer:

_____

_____

You now have the beginning of a side hustle idea. Repeat this process with more skills to generate additional possibilities.

C) Quick Brainstorm Table

Use this table to come up with multiple side hustle ideas. Do not evaluate them yet. You will validate them in the next section.

Worksheet: Quick Brainstorm Table

Skill or Passion	Problem Solved	Result Delivered	Possible Offer Idea

Leave room for five to ten entries. Fill the table without judging your ideas. Quantity matters more than perfection here.

You are not trying to find a perfect offer. You are gathering options so you can test the strongest one.

D) Final Spark Questions

If you feel stuck, use these questions to generate one more idea:

• What could I do for someone in one hour

• What could I deliver in one week

• What could I teach in a short lesson, tutorial, or mini coaching session

• What small physical or digital product could I create in a limited batch

• What task do people avoid, struggle with, or dislike that I could do more easily

Your next idea might be something simple enough that you can start with it immediately.

> Any idea can grow later. For now, focus on a simple version that someone can buy quickly. Clarity creates confidence. Small ideas often lead to big results.

Chapter 5
Validation Checklist
Is it worth pursuing?

Before you build anything, you need to make sure your idea is worth your time. Validation helps you confirm that people want your solution and are willing to pay for it. Your goal is not to guess. Your goal is to gather proof. This checklist will show whether your idea has strong potential, needs adjustment, or should be replaced.

A) How to Use This Checklist

You will evaluate your idea based on four areas:

1 Demand - Are people actively looking for this solution

2 Value - Does this idea solve a meaningful problem

3 Profit - Can this earn money without heavy cost or effort

4 Fit - Is this idea right for your skills and your lifestyle

Answer each question with **Yes** or **No** only. Honest answers lead to better decisions.

B) Validation Questions

Demand

Check for clear evidence that people want what you offer.

Have people paid for something similar before

Yes ☐ No ☐

Do people complain about this problem online or offline

Yes ☐ No ☐

Can you easily find people who would want this solution

Yes ☐ No ☐

Is there a specific group who clearly needs this, not just everyone

Yes ☐ No ☐

Value

Value comes from solving a problem that feels important.

Does this save someone time, stress, or effort

Yes ☐ No ☐

Does this help someone reach a goal or finish something faster

Yes ☐ No ☐

Would someone feel relief, pride, or satisfaction afterward

Yes ☐ No ☐

Can the benefit be explained in a few simple sentences

Yes ☐ No ☐

Profit

Strong ideas can start earning quickly without high costs.

Can you deliver a basic version without spending much money

Yes ☐ No ☐

Can you deliver a basic version within a short time

Yes ☐ No ☐

Could you test a small version first to avoid risk

Yes ☐ No ☐

Can the offer improve over time without being rebuilt from zero

Yes ☐ No ☐

Fit

A profitable idea must match your personality, comfort, and lifestyle.

Do you already have the skill or can you learn it quickly

Yes ☐ No ☐

Would you feel comfortable offering this to customers

Yes ☐ No ☐

Would you still enjoy this work if you did it for others

Yes ☐ No ☐

Could you do this consistently without stress or resentment

Yes ☐ No ☐

C) Simple Scoring Guide

Count all your Yes answers.

If you score:

14 to 16 Yes

Your idea is strong. It is worth pursuing.

10 to 13 Yes

Worth testing, but begin with a small, simple version.

Under 10 Yes

Needs more research or a different approach before moving forward.

Honest No answers can save you weeks of wasted effort. This is progress, not failure.

D) Red Flags to Notice

A single No in any of these areas should make you pause:

- The problem is not clear
- No one pays for similar solutions
- It would take weeks or high cost to create a small version
- You would not enjoy doing this repeatedly

If any of these are true, you may need to adjust your idea before continuing.

E) Final Decision Box

After reviewing your answers, select one:

☐ **Yes, this idea is worth pursuing**

☐ **Yes, but I will start with a small test version**

☐ **Not yet, it needs adjustments**

☐ **No, I should explore a different idea**

My Next Action

Write your immediate next step based on your choice above.

Next action: _____

_____

_____

_____

_____

Chapter 6

90-Day Goal Roadmap

Outcome goals, weekly
targets, income target

The next ninety days will transform your idea into income. This roadmap helps you set clear results, choose practical money goals, and break them into weekly targets that guide your daily actions. Your focus is not on doing more. Your focus is on doing the right actions that lead to customers and revenue.

A) Outcome Goals

Outcome goals describe the results you want in ninety days. They do not list tasks. Instead, they describe the impact you want to make, the value you want to deliver, and the changes you want to see in your business.

Outcome Goal Prompts

Answer the following to define your results: (you can use a seperate notebook or the blank pages at the back of this planner)

1. What result do you want from your side hustle in the next ninety days?

2. What problem will your offer help customers solve?

3. What success would look like three months from now?

4. What type of feedback or testimonials would you like to receive?

5. What business milestone would make you feel proud?

Write your answers clearly so you know exactly where you are going.

Outcome Goal Boxes

Use these sections to define your outcomes.

Primary outcome goal:
This is the most important result you want in the next ninety days.

_____

_____

_____

Customer or product outcome:
This describes the change you want your offer to deliver to others.

_____

_____

_____

Personal growth outcome:
This describes who you want to become through this process.

_____

_____

_____

_____

. . .

Outcome *goals show direction.* & *Your actions will create the results.*

B) Income Target

Healthy income goals are based on the first version of your offer, not the perfect future version. Your goal is to earn steadily, learn from customers, and grow with data.

Income Target Prompts

Answer to set realistic expectations:

1. How much income do you want your side hustle to produce in ninety days?

2. How many people need to buy for you to reach that amount?

3. What price or price range supports this goal without undervaluing your time?

Income Target Worksheet

Item or Service	Price	Sales Needed	Expected Revenue

Total ninety day income target: _____

Minimum number of sales needed: _____

The goal is consistent income, not perfect income. Small profits grow when you focus on simple repeatable actions.

C) Weekly Targets

Weekly targets break the ninety day plan into simple actions that guide your daily tasks. These are the most important steps that lead you to income. Daily work supports these weekly goals.

Weekly Target Prompts

Use these questions to choose strong weekly goals:

1. What action builds or improves my offer?

2. What action brings potential customers to me?

3. What action supports pricing, clarity, or delivery?

Monthly Breakdown

Use this table as a guide or create your own targets based on your offer.

Month	Weekly Target 1	Weekly Target 2	Weekly Target 3	Weekly Target 4
Month 1	Choose and validate ideas	Customer research tasks	Pricing check tasks	Choose final offer
Month 2	Create simple version	Set payment method	Write sales message	Launch to first customers
Month 3	Improve offer	Promote regularly	Track income and time	Add one marketing habit

Rewrite these to match your validated idea if needed.

Weekly targets guide your progress. Daily tasks support these targets, not the other way around.

D) Success Indicators

Success is not only measured by income. It is measured by actions that lead to income. These indicators show that your business is growing in the right direction.

Success Indicator List

Check off each one as it happens.

- ☐ I received interest or inquiries about my offer
- ☐ I collected real feedback from potential customers
- ☐ I gained at least one paying customer
- ☐ Someone asked about price or availability
- ☐ I created something that can be delivered
- ☐ I repeated one weekly marketing habit
- ☐ I raised or confirmed my pricing with confidence
- ☐ I improved the offer based on customer insight

Progress Check Box

Mark here when you feel momentum:

☐ I am making progress toward steady income

Progress is measured by consistent actions that lead to customers. Income follows action.

Your Roadmap is Ready

You now have a ninety day plan with outcomes, income goals, and weekly targets that turn effort into results. Keep it simple. Focus on key actions. Build, learn, and earn step by step.

Part 2

12 Weekly Sections

Chapter 7
Week 1: Begin

This page helps you begin each week with clarity. Your goal is to focus on the few actions that move your side hustle forward. Write short, specific answers that you can act on daily.

This Week's Focus

What is the single most important result you want by the end of this week?

My weekly focus:

This Week's Top Three Goals

Choose three goals that directly support your focus. These must be outcomes, not tasks.

1

2

3

Before choosing tasks, make sure each goal leads to progress you can measure or deliver.

Key Action Steps

Break each goal into actions you can complete this week. Keep them clear and simple.

- Goal 1 action steps:

- Goal 2 action steps:

- Goal 3 action steps:

Customer Connection Plan

How will you connect with people who need your offer this week

Think messages, research, sharing value, asking questions, or inviting interest.

Plan to connect:

Time Commitment

How much time will you dedicate this week

Choose a realistic schedule you can promise yourself.

I will commit:

□ 10 to 30 minutes daily

□ 45 to 60 minutes daily

□ Certain days only: _____

Success Reminder

Write a short sentence that describes success for this week. Keep it inspiring and specific.

Success for me this week means:

Weekly Action Plan Checklist

You may use this checklist throughout your side hustle journey, these actions create real progress whether you are choosing your idea, building your offer, or selling it. Mark off tasks as you complete them and aim for consistency, not perfection.

1. Build or Improve the Offer

Your product or service becomes stronger when you work on it a little at a time.

☐ I worked on something customers will receive

☐ I improved one step or feature of my offer

☐ I simplified or removed something that was not needed

☐ I prepared a version that can be delivered faster or easier

> Progress means improving what exists, not adding more work.

2. Connect With Real People

Talking to people helps you understand what they need and how you can help.

☐ I asked questions to learn what people struggle with

☐ I started a conversation about a need or problem

☐ I listened to feedback or concerns

☐ I invited someone to learn more about my offer

> Connection is more valuable than followers or likes.

3. Promote With Purpose

Customers need reminders, clarity, and visibility. Promotion helps them see how you can help.

☐ I shared what problem I solve

☐ I explained the result my offer delivers

☐ I told people how to buy or book

☐ I posted, messaged, or shared something helpful and relevant

People cannot buy what they cannot see clearly.

4. Track Time and Money

Tracking creates honest awareness. Awareness creates smarter decisions.

☐ I tracked time spent on my business

☐ I tracked expenses or materials used

☐ I recorded income or potential leads

☐ I noted where effort produced the best results

Better tracking leads to better pricing and better profit.

5. Learn One Thing that Makes You Better

Growth does not require long study sessions. One useful insight each week is enough.

☐ I learned from customer feedback

☐ I studied a question or topic related to my niche

☐ I observed what competitors are doing well

☐ I practiced a skill that helps my delivery or promotion

Mini insight of the week:

Learning is only useful when combined with action.

Weekly Completion Check

☐ I completed the actions that matter most

☐ I moved closer to income through simple steps

☐ I worked consistently rather than trying to be perfect

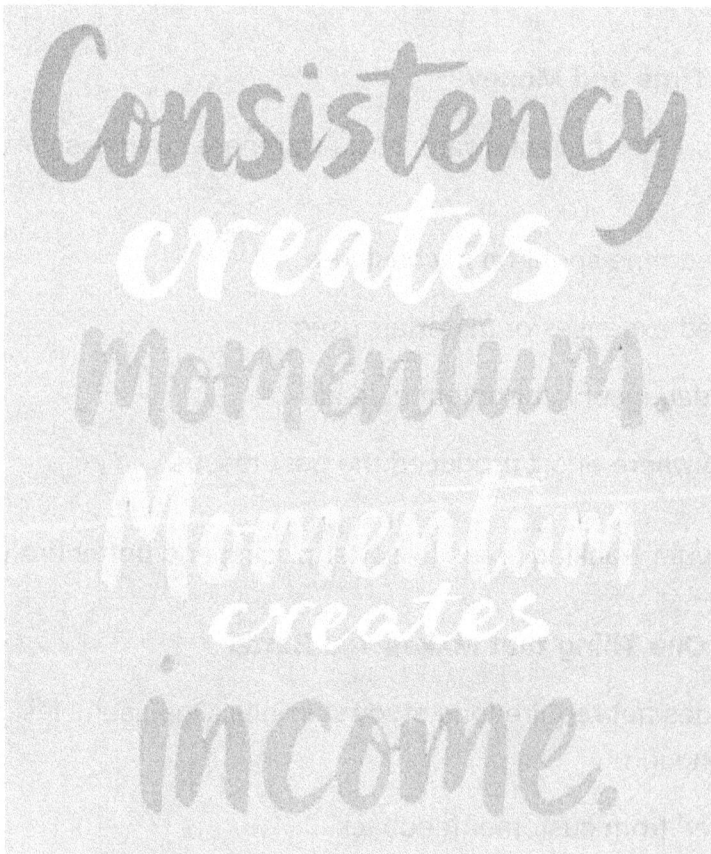

Mini Learning Prompt

Each week, take a few minutes to learn something that makes your business stronger. The goal is not to study endlessly. The goal is to gain one insight that helps you sell, deliver, or improve your offer. Use this page to focus your learning and turn knowledge into action.

This Week's Question

Choose one question that helps you understand your market, your offer, or your customer. You can write your own or pick from the list below.

My learning question of the week:

Ideas for Learning Questions

Pick one if you need inspiration.

- What result do people want most from my offer
- What frustrates customers about current solutions
- What small improvement would make my offer more valuable
- What type of content or message gets the most attention
- What do customers complain about in my niche
- What topics do people ask questions about again and again

- How do others in my niche describe the problem I solve

- What skill could I improve that would increase my value

- What do successful sellers do that I can learn from

- How could I deliver my product or service faster or more clearly

What I Discovered

Write your insight in one to three sentences. Keep it clear and practical.

My learning insight:

How I Will Use This Insight

Learning matters only when it leads to action. Choose a small step you can take based on what you learned.

One change or improvement I will make:?

Every week you learn something useful, you become more valuable. More value creates more income.

Weekly Budget and Cost Tracker

Strong businesses manage money from the start. This page helps you track what you spend and what you earn during the week. You are learning how to make profit without high costs or guesswork.

Weekly Budget Plan

Plan your spending before the week starts. Keep it lean and practical. Only spend money that supports profit or delivery.

Planned spending this week:

What will I invest in and why

(example: materials, tools, ads, packaging)

Spend for value, not for excitement. Simple solutions often cost less and work better.

Cost Breakdown

List any expenses that support your side hustle. Include business tools, supplies, shipping, packaging, digital tools, ads, or delivery costs.

Date

Expense Item

Purpose

Cost

Total spent this week: _____

. . .

Income Received

List any income earned from products, services, or pre orders.

Date

Customer or Order

Product or Service

Amount

Total income this week: _____

Profit and Results

Calculate your weekly outcome.

Profit or loss this week

Income minus expenses: _____

How this week helped my business

Reflect on what worked financially.

☐ I kept costs low

☐ I improved how I price

☐ I created value without overspending

☐ I learned what customers respond to

☐ I focused on smart investments

Savings and Future Planning

If you saved money this week, note how you will use it in the future.

Savings or remaining budget: _____

**Next week financial
adjustment:_____**

Smart spending
builds
profit
Profit grows

your business steadely

Weekly Marketing Task

Choose one strategic marketing action this week. The goal is to share your offer with clarity and intention so people know how you can help them. Pick a single task and complete it before the week ends.

This Week's Marketing Task

Write one clear promotional action. Keep it specific.

My task:

Who Is This For

Identify the type of person this message or action is meant to reach.

Target audience:

What Value Will I Share

Explain the benefit, result, or helpful insight you will communicate.

Value or benefit:

Where Will I Share It

Choose the place or method. Examples include a post, story, message, email, conversation, group, or platform.

☐ Social post

☐ Direct message

☐ Community group

☐ Short video

☐ Email

☐ In person

☐ Other: _____

What Is the Call to Action

Tell people what to do next. Example: message you, ask a question, buy, book, request more info.

Call to action:

Follow Up and Results

After completing the task, fill in your results.

How many people engaged or responded

What questions did people ask

What worked well about this message

What I will try or repeat next week

●————————●

Marketing works through clarity and repetition, not pressure. Real questions, real value, and real conversations lead to sales.

Weekly Review and Sales Reflection

At the end of each week, pause and check what you learned, what you earned, and what you can improve. This reflection helps you build a stronger offer without working harder. Focus on real progress, not perfection.

Weekly Wins

List anything that worked well, big or small. Wins include effort, actions, conversations, clarity, and sales.

This week

I am proud of:

Customer Insight

People teach you what they value. Write any feedback, questions, compliments, problems, or requests you heard this week.

Feedback or insights from real people:

Sales Reflection

Answer these honestly to build smarter habits.

• Did I make an offer or invite someone to buy

Yes ☐ No ☐

• Did anyone ask about my product, price, or service

Yes ☐ No ☐

• Did I earn income this week

Yes ☐ No ☐

If yes, write how much:

Income earned: _____

If no, write what you will do differently:

Adjustment next week: _____

Time and Effort Check

How consistent were you this week

☐ I worked each day I planned

☐ I worked on fewer days than planned

☐ I did not follow my plan but learned something useful

Total time spent: _____ hours or minutes

What to Improve

Reflect on one small change that could make next week better. Improvement means simplifying, not adding more work.

One change I will make next week:

Next Week Action Boost

Choose one habit to repeat for better results next week.

☐ Share customer feedback

☐ Promote my offer once per day

☐ Reach out to potential customers

☐ Track time and income daily

☐ Improve my product or service

Chapter 8
Week 2: Discover

This page helps you begin each week with clarity. Your goal is to focus on the few actions that move your side hustle forward. Write short, specific answers that you can act on daily.

This Week's Focus

What is the single most important result you want by the end of this week?

My weekly focus:

This Week's Top Three Goals

Choose three goals that directly support your focus. These must be outcomes, not tasks.

1

2

3

Before choosing tasks, make sure each goal leads to progress you can measure or deliver.

Key Action Steps

Break each goal into actions you can complete this week. Keep them clear and simple.

• Goal 1 action steps:

• Goal 2 action steps:

• Goal 3 action steps:

Customer Connection Plan

How will you connect with people who need your offer this week

Think messages, research, sharing value, asking questions, or inviting interest.

Plan to connect:

Time Commitment

How much time will you dedicate this week

Choose a realistic schedule you can promise yourself.

I will commit:

☐ 10 to 30 minutes daily

☐ 45 to 60 minutes daily

☐ Certain days only: _____

Success Reminder

Write a short sentence that describes success for this week. Keep it inspiring and specific.

Success for me this week means:

Weekly Action Plan Checklist

You may use this checklist throughout your side hustle journey, these actions create real progress whether you are choosing your idea, building your offer, or selling it. Mark off tasks as you complete them and aim for consistency, not perfection.

1. Build or Improve the Offer

Your product or service becomes stronger when you work on it a little at a time.

☐ I worked on something customers will receive

☐ I improved one step or feature of my offer

☐ I simplified or removed something that was not needed

☐ I prepared a version that can be delivered faster or easier

> Progress means improving what exists, not adding more work.

2. Connect With Real People

Talking to people helps you understand what they need and how you can help.

☐ I asked questions to learn what people struggle with

☐ I started a conversation about a need or problem

☐ I listened to feedback or concerns

☐ I invited someone to learn more about my offer

> Connection is more valuable than followers or likes.

3. Promote With Purpose

Customers need reminders, clarity, and visibility. Promotion helps them see how you can help.

☐ I shared what problem I solve

☐ I explained the result my offer delivers

☐ I told people how to buy or book

☐ I posted, messaged, or shared something helpful and relevant

People cannot buy what they cannot see clearly.

4. Track Time and Money

Tracking creates honest awareness. Awareness creates smarter decisions.

☐ I tracked time spent on my business

☐ I tracked expenses or materials used

☐ I recorded income or potential leads

☐ I noted where effort produced the best results

Better tracking leads to better pricing and better profit.

5. Learn One Thing that Makes You Better

Growth does not require long study sessions. One useful insight each week is enough.

☐ I learned from customer feedback

☐ I studied a question or topic related to my niche

☐ I observed what competitors are doing well

☐ I practiced a skill that helps my delivery or promotion

Mini insight of the week:

Learning is only useful when combined with action.

Weekly Completion Check

☐ I completed the actions that matter most

☐ I moved closer to income through simple steps

☐ I worked consistently rather than trying to be perfect

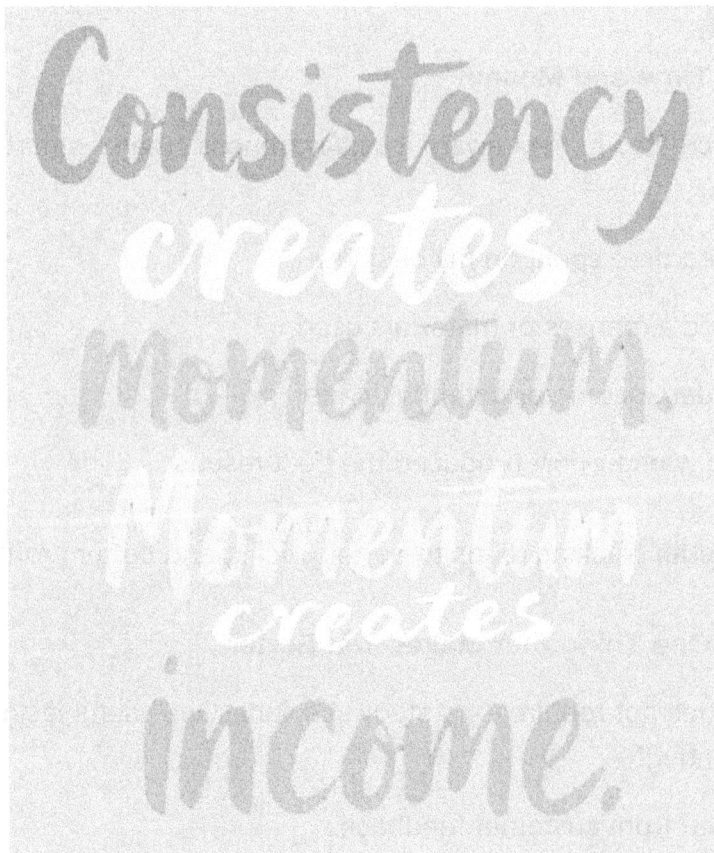

Consistency creates momentum. Momentum creates income.

Mini Learning Prompt

Each week, take a few minutes to learn something that makes your business stronger. The goal is not to study endlessly. The goal is to gain one insight that helps you sell, deliver, or improve your offer. Use this page to focus your learning and turn knowledge into action.

This Week's Question

Choose one question that helps you understand your market, your offer, or your customer. You can write your own or pick from the list below.

My learning question of the week:

Ideas for Learning Questions

Pick one if you need inspiration.

- What result do people want most from my offer

- What frustrates customers about current solutions

- What small improvement would make my offer more valuable

- What type of content or message gets the most attention

- What do customers complain about in my niche

- What topics do people ask questions about again and again

- How do others in my niche describe the problem I solve

- What skill could I improve that would increase my value

- What do successful sellers do that I can learn from

- How could I deliver my product or service faster or more clearly

What I Discovered

Write your insight in one to three sentences. Keep it clear and practical.

My learning insight:

How I Will Use This Insight

Learning matters only when it leads to action. Choose a small step you can take based on what you learned.

One change or improvement I will make:?

Every week you learn something useful, you become more valuable. More value creates more income.

Weekly Budget and Cost Tracker

Strong businesses manage money from the start. This page helps you track what you spend and what you earn during the week. You are learning how to make profit without high costs or guesswork.

Weekly Budget Plan

Plan your spending before the week starts. Keep it lean and practical. Only spend money that supports profit or delivery.

Planned spending this week:

What will I invest in and why

(example: materials, tools, ads, packaging)

Spend for value, not for excitement. Simple solutions often cost less and work better.

Cost Breakdown

List any expenses that support your side hustle. Include business tools, supplies, shipping, packaging, digital tools, ads, or delivery costs.

Date

Expense Item

Purpose

Cost

Total spent this week: _____

· · ·

Income Received

List any income earned from products, services, or pre orders.

Date

Customer or Order

Product or Service

Amount

Total income this week: _____

Profit and Results

Calculate your weekly outcome.

Profit or loss this week

Income minus expenses: _____

How this week helped my business

Reflect on what worked financially.

☐ I kept costs low

☐ I improved how I price

☐ I created value without overspending

☐ I learned what customers respond to

☐ I focused on smart investments

Savings and Future Planning

If you saved money this week, note how you will use it in the future.

Savings or remaining budget: _____

Next week financial
adjustment:_____

Smart spending
builds
profit
Profit grows
your business steadely

Weekly Marketing Task

Choose one strategic marketing action this week. The goal is to share your offer with clarity and intention so people know how you can help them. Pick a single task and complete it before the week ends.

This Week's Marketing Task

Write one clear promotional action. Keep it specific.

My task:

Who Is This For

Identify the type of person this message or action is meant to reach.

Target audience:

What Value Will I Share

Explain the benefit, result, or helpful insight you will communicate.

Value or benefit:

Where Will I Share It

Choose the place or method. Examples include a post, story, message, email, conversation, group, or platform.

☐ Social post

☐ Direct message

☐ Community group

☐ Short video

☐ Email

☐ In person

☐ Other: _____

What Is the Call to Action

Tell people what to do next. Example: message you, ask a question, buy, book, request more info.

Call to action:

Follow Up and Results

After completing the task, fill in your results.

How many people engaged or responded

What questions did people ask

What worked well about this message

What I will try or repeat next week

● ———————— ●

Marketing works through clarity and repetition, not pressure. Real questions, real value, and real conversations lead to sales.

Weekly Review and Sales Reflection

At the end of each week, pause and check what you learned, what you earned, and what you can improve. This reflection helps you build a stronger offer without working harder. Focus on real progress, not perfection.

Weekly Wins

List anything that worked well, big or small. Wins include effort, actions, conversations, clarity, and sales.

This week

I am proud of:

Customer Insight

People teach you what they value. Write any feedback, questions, compliments, problems, or requests you heard this week.

Feedback or insights from real people:

Sales Reflection

Answer these honestly to build smarter habits.

• Did I make an offer or invite someone to buy

Yes ☐ No ☐

• Did anyone ask about my product, price, or service

Yes ☐ No ☐

• Did I earn income this week

Yes ☐ No ☐

If yes, write how much:

Income earned: _____

If no, write what you will do differently:

Adjustment next week: _____

Time and Effort Check

How consistent were you this week

☐ I worked each day I planned

☐ I worked on fewer days than planned

☐ I did not follow my plan but learned something useful

Total time spent: _____ hours or minutes

What to Improve

Reflect on one small change that could make next week better. Improvement means simplifying, not adding more work.

One change I will make next week:

Next Week Action Boost

Choose one habit to repeat for better results next week.

☐ Share customer feedback

☐ Promote my offer once per day

☐ Reach out to potential customers

☐ Track time and income daily

☐ Improve my product or service

Chapter 9
Week 3: Explore

This page helps you begin each week with clarity. Your goal is to focus on the few actions that move your side hustle forward. Write short, specific answers that you can act on daily.

This Week's Focus

What is the single most important result you want by the end of this week?

My weekly focus:

This Week's Top Three Goals

Choose three goals that directly support your focus. These must be outcomes, not tasks.

1

2

3

Before choosing tasks, make sure each goal leads to progress you can measure or deliver.

Key Action Steps

Break each goal into actions you can complete this week. Keep them clear and simple.

• Goal 1 action steps:

• Goal 2 action steps:

• Goal 3 action steps:

Customer Connection Plan

How will you connect with people who need your offer this week

Think messages, research, sharing value, asking questions, or inviting interest.

Plan to connect:

Time Commitment

How much time will you dedicate this week

Choose a realistic schedule you can promise yourself.

I will commit:

☐ 10 to 30 minutes daily

☐ 45 to 60 minutes daily

☐ Certain days only: _____

Success Reminder

Write a short sentence that describes success for this week. Keep it inspiring and specific.

Success for me this week means:

Weekly Action Plan Checklist

You may use this checklist throughout your side hustle journey, these actions create real progress whether you are choosing your idea, building your offer, or selling it. Mark off tasks as you complete them and aim for consistency, not perfection.

1. Build or Improve the Offer

Your product or service becomes stronger when you work on it a little at a time.

☐ I worked on something customers will receive

☐ I improved one step or feature of my offer

☐ I simplified or removed something that was not needed

☐ I prepared a version that can be delivered faster or easier

> Progress means improving what exists, not adding more work.

2. Connect With Real People

Talking to people helps you understand what they need and how you can help.

☐ I asked questions to learn what people struggle with

☐ I started a conversation about a need or problem

☐ I listened to feedback or concerns

☐ I invited someone to learn more about my offer

> Connection is more valuable than followers or likes.

3. Promote With Purpose

Customers need reminders, clarity, and visibility. Promotion helps them see how you can help.

☐ I shared what problem I solve

☐ I explained the result my offer delivers

☐ I told people how to buy or book

☐ I posted, messaged, or shared something helpful and relevant

People cannot buy what they cannot see clearly.

4. Track Time and Money

Tracking creates honest awareness. Awareness creates smarter decisions.

☐ I tracked time spent on my business

☐ I tracked expenses or materials used

☐ I recorded income or potential leads

☐ I noted where effort produced the best results

Better tracking leads to better pricing and better profit.

5. Learn One Thing that Makes You Better

Growth does not require long study sessions. One useful insight each week is enough.

☐ I learned from customer feedback

☐ I studied a question or topic related to my niche

☐ I observed what competitors are doing well

☐ I practiced a skill that helps my delivery or promotion

Mini insight of the week:

Learning is only useful when combined with action.

Weekly Completion Check

☐ I completed the actions that matter most

☐ I moved closer to income through simple steps

☐ I worked consistently rather than trying to be perfect

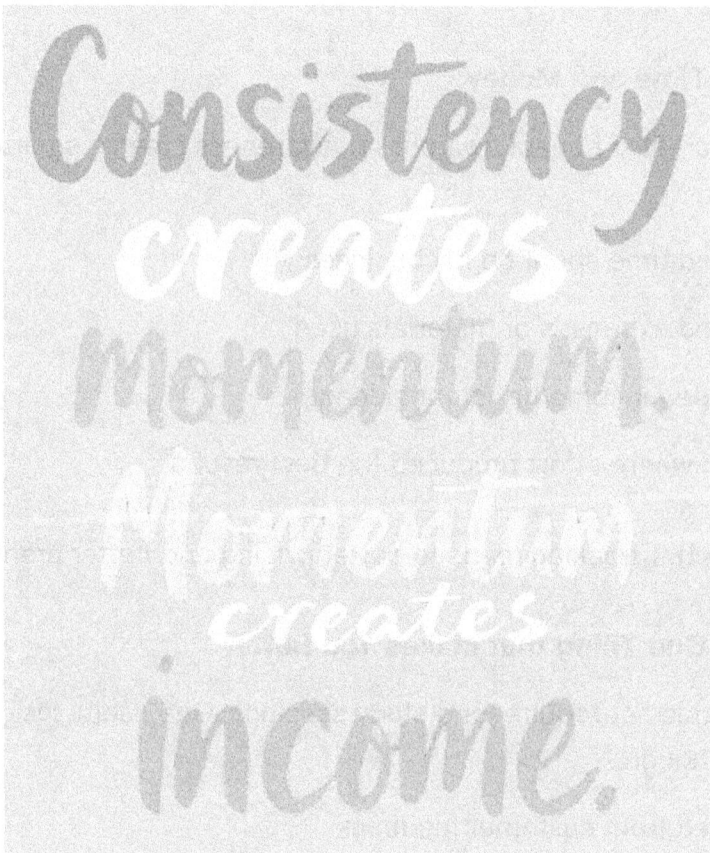

Mini Learning Prompt

Each week, take a few minutes to learn something that makes your business stronger. The goal is not to study endlessly. The goal is to gain one insight that helps you sell, deliver, or improve your offer. Use this page to focus your learning and turn knowledge into action.

This Week's Question

Choose one question that helps you understand your market, your offer, or your customer. You can write your own or pick from the list below.

My learning question of the week:

Ideas for Learning Questions

Pick one if you need inspiration.

- What result do people want most from my offer

- What frustrates customers about current solutions

- What small improvement would make my offer more valuable

- What type of content or message gets the most attention

- What do customers complain about in my niche

- What topics do people ask questions about again and again

- How do others in my niche describe the problem I solve

- What skill could I improve that would increase my value

- What do successful sellers do that I can learn from

- How could I deliver my product or service faster or more clearly

What I Discovered

Write your insight in one to three sentences. Keep it clear and practical.

My learning insight:

How I Will Use This Insight

Learning matters only when it leads to action. Choose a small step you can take based on what you learned.

One change or improvement I will make:?

_____

Every week you learn something useful, you become more valuable. More value creates more income.

Weekly Budget and Cost Tracker

Strong businesses manage money from the start. This page helps you track what you spend and what you earn during the week. You are learning how to make profit without high costs or guesswork.

Weekly Budget Plan

Plan your spending before the week starts. Keep it lean and practical. Only spend money that supports profit or delivery.

Planned spending this week:

What will I invest in and why

(example: materials, tools, ads, packaging)

Spend for value, not for excitement. Simple solutions often cost less and work better.

Cost Breakdown

List any expenses that support your side hustle. Include business tools, supplies, shipping, packaging, digital tools, ads, or delivery costs.

Date

Expense Item

Purpose

Cost

Total spent this week: _____

. . .

Income Received

List any income earned from products, services, or pre orders.

Date

Customer or Order

Product or Service

Amount

Total income this week: _____

Profit and Results

Calculate your weekly outcome.

Profit or loss this week

Income minus expenses: _____

How this week helped my business

Reflect on what worked financially.

☐ I kept costs low

☐ I improved how I price

☐ I created value without overspending

☐ I learned what customers respond to

☐ I focused on smart investments

Savings and Future Planning

If you saved money this week, note how you will use it in the future.

Savings or remaining budget: _____

Next week financial adjustment:_____

Smart spending builds profit

Profit grows

your business steadely

Weekly Marketing Task

Choose one strategic marketing action this week. The goal is to share your offer with clarity and intention so people know how you can help them. Pick a single task and complete it before the week ends.

This Week's Marketing Task

Write one clear promotional action. Keep it specific.

My task:

Who Is This For

Identify the type of person this message or action is meant to reach.

Target audience:

What Value Will I Share

Explain the benefit, result, or helpful insight you will communicate.

Value or benefit:

Where Will I Share It

Choose the place or method. Examples include a post, story, message, email, conversation, group, or platform.

☐ Social post

☐ Direct message

☐ Community group

☐ Short video

☐ Email

☐ In person

☐ Other: _____

What Is the Call to Action

Tell people what to do next. Example: message you, ask a question, buy, book, request more info.

Call to action:

Follow Up and Results

After completing the task, fill in your results.

How many people engaged or responded

What questions did people ask

What worked well about this message

What I will try or repeat next week

● ——————— ●

Marketing works through clarity and repetition, not pressure. Real questions, real value, and real conversations lead to sales.

Weekly Review and Sales Reflection

At the end of each week, pause and check what you learned, what you earned, and what you can improve. This reflection helps you build a stronger offer without working harder. Focus on real progress, not perfection.

Weekly Wins

List anything that worked well, big or small. Wins include effort, actions, conversations, clarity, and sales.

This week

I am proud of:

Customer Insight

People teach you what they value. Write any feedback, questions, compliments, problems, or requests you heard this week.

Feedback or insights from real people:

Sales Reflection

Answer these honestly to build smarter habits.

• Did I make an offer or invite someone to buy

Yes ☐ No ☐

• Did anyone ask about my product, price, or service

Yes ☐ No ☐

• Did I earn income this week

Yes ☐ No ☐

If yes, write how much:

Income earned: _____

If no, write what you will do differently:

Adjustment next week: _____

Time and Effort Check

How consistent were you this week

☐ I worked each day I planned

☐ I worked on fewer days than planned

☐ I did not follow my plan but learned something useful

Total time spent: _____ hours or minutes

What to Improve

Reflect on one small change that could make next week better. Improvement means simplifying, not adding more work.

One change I will make next week:

Next Week Action Boost

Choose one habit to repeat for better results next week.

☐ Share customer feedback

☐ Promote my offer once per day

☐ Reach out to potential customers

☐ Track time and income daily

☐ Improve my product or service

Chapter 10
Week 4: Decide

This page helps you begin each week with clarity. Your goal is to focus on the few actions that move your side hustle forward. Write short, specific answers that you can act on daily.

This Week's Focus

What is the single most important result you want by the end of this week?

My weekly focus:

This Week's Top Three Goals

Choose three goals that directly support your focus. These must be outcomes, not tasks.

1

2

3

Before choosing tasks, make sure each goal leads to progress you can measure or deliver.

Key Action Steps

Break each goal into actions you can complete this week. Keep them clear and simple.

• Goal 1 action steps:

• Goal 2 action steps:

• Goal 3 action steps:

Customer Connection Plan

How will you connect with people who need your offer this week

Think messages, research, sharing value, asking questions, or inviting interest.

Plan to connect:

Time Commitment

How much time will you dedicate this week

Choose a realistic schedule you can promise yourself.

I will commit:

☐ 10 to 30 minutes daily

☐ 45 to 60 minutes daily

☐ Certain days only: _____

Success Reminder

Write a short sentence that describes success for this week. Keep it inspiring and specific.

Success for me this week means:

Weekly Action Plan Checklist

You may use this checklist throughout your side hustle journey, these actions create real progress whether you are choosing your idea, building your offer, or selling it. Mark off tasks as you complete them and aim for consistency, not perfection.

1. Build or Improve the Offer

Your product or service becomes stronger when you work on it a little at a time.

☐ I worked on something customers will receive

☐ I improved one step or feature of my offer

☐ I simplified or removed something that was not needed

☐ I prepared a version that can be delivered faster or easier

> Progress means improving what exists, not adding more work.

2. Connect With Real People

Talking to people helps you understand what they need and how you can help.

☐ I asked questions to learn what people struggle with

☐ I started a conversation about a need or problem

☐ I listened to feedback or concerns

☐ I invited someone to learn more about my offer

> Connection is more valuable than followers or likes.

3. Promote With Purpose

Customers need reminders, clarity, and visibility. Promotion helps them see how you can help.

☐ I shared what problem I solve

☐ I explained the result my offer delivers

☐ I told people how to buy or book

☐ I posted, messaged, or shared something helpful and relevant

People cannot buy what they cannot see clearly.

4. Track Time and Money

Tracking creates honest awareness. Awareness creates smarter decisions.

☐ I tracked time spent on my business

☐ I tracked expenses or materials used

☐ I recorded income or potential leads

☐ I noted where effort produced the best results

Better tracking leads to better pricing and better profit.

5. Learn One Thing that Makes You Better

Growth does not require long study sessions. One useful insight each week is enough.

☐ I learned from customer feedback

☐ I studied a question or topic related to my niche

☐ I observed what competitors are doing well

☐ I practiced a skill that helps my delivery or promotion

Mini insight of the week:

Learning is only useful when combined with action.

Weekly Completion Check

☐ I completed the actions that matter most

☐ I moved closer to income through simple steps

☐ I worked consistently rather than trying to be perfect

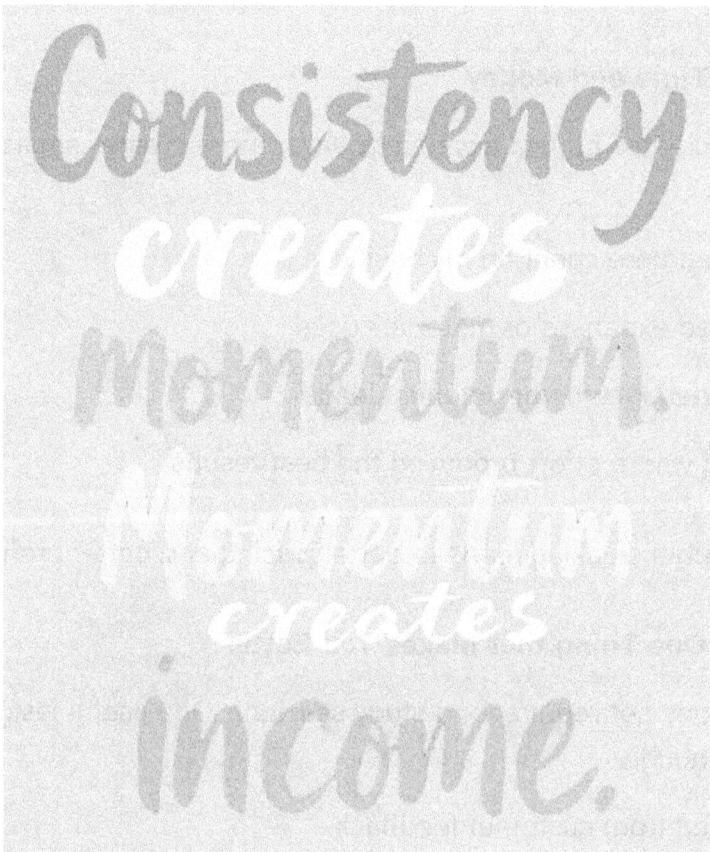

.

Mini Learning Prompt

Each week, take a few minutes to learn something that makes your business stronger. The goal is not to study endlessly. The goal is to gain one insight that helps you sell, deliver, or improve your offer. Use this page to focus your learning and turn knowledge into action.

This Week's Question

Choose one question that helps you understand your market, your offer, or your customer. You can write your own or pick from the list below.

My learning question of the week:

Ideas for Learning Questions

Pick one if you need inspiration.

- What result do people want most from my offer

- What frustrates customers about current solutions

- What small improvement would make my offer more valuable

- What type of content or message gets the most attention

- What do customers complain about in my niche

- What topics do people ask questions about again and again

- How do others in my niche describe the problem I solve

- What skill could I improve that would increase my value

- What do successful sellers do that I can learn from

- How could I deliver my product or service faster or more clearly

What I Discovered

Write your insight in one to three sentences. Keep it clear and practical.

My learning insight:

How I Will Use This Insight

Learning matters only when it leads to action. Choose a small step you can take based on what you learned.

One change or improvement I will make:?

_____

Every week you learn something useful, you become more valuable. More value creates more income.

Weekly Budget and Cost Tracker

Strong businesses manage money from the start. This page helps you track what you spend and what you earn during the week. You are learning how to make profit without high costs or guesswork.

Weekly Budget Plan

Plan your spending before the week starts. Keep it lean and practical. Only spend money that supports profit or delivery.

Planned spending this week:

What will I invest in and why

(example: materials, tools, ads, packaging)

Spend for value, not for excitement. Simple solutions often cost less and work better.

Cost Breakdown

List any expenses that support your side hustle. Include business tools, supplies, shipping, packaging, digital tools, ads, or delivery costs.

Date

Expense Item

Purpose

Cost

Total spent this week: _____

. . .

Income Received

List any income earned from products, services, or pre orders.

Date

Customer or Order

Product or Service

Amount

Total income this week: _____

Profit and Results

Calculate your weekly outcome.

Profit or loss this week

Income minus expenses: _____

How this week helped my business

Reflect on what worked financially.

☐ I kept costs low

☐ I improved how I price

☐ I created value without overspending

☐ I learned what customers respond to

☐ I focused on smart investments

Savings and Future Planning

If you saved money this week, note how you will use it in the future.

Savings or remaining budget: _____

**Next week financial
adjustment:**_____

Smart spending
builds
profit
Profit grows
your business steadely

Weekly Marketing Task

Choose one strategic marketing action this week. The goal is to share your offer with clarity and intention so people know how you can help them. Pick a single task and complete it before the week ends.

This Week's Marketing Task

Write one clear promotional action. Keep it specific.

My task:

Who Is This For

Identify the type of person this message or action is meant to reach.

Target audience:

What Value Will I Share

Explain the benefit, result, or helpful insight you will communicate.

Value or benefit:

Where Will I Share It

Choose the place or method. Examples include a post, story, message, email, conversation, group, or platform.

☐ Social post

☐ Direct message

☐ Community group

☐ Short video

☐ Email

☐ In person

☐ Other: _____

What Is the Call to Action

Tell people what to do next. Example: message you, ask a question, buy, book, request more info.

Call to action:

Follow Up and Results

After completing the task, fill in your results.

How many people engaged or responded

What questions did people ask

What worked well about this message

What I will try or repeat next week

●———————————●

Marketing works through clarity and repetition, not pressure. Real questions, real value, and real conversations lead to sales.

Weekly Review and Sales Reflection

At the end of each week, pause and check what you learned, what you earned, and what you can improve. This reflection helps you build a stronger offer without working harder. Focus on real progress, not perfection.

Weekly Wins

List anything that worked well, big or small. Wins include effort, actions, conversations, clarity, and sales.

This week

I am proud of:

Customer Insight

People teach you what they value. Write any feedback, questions, compliments, problems, or requests you heard this week.

Feedback or insights from real people:

Sales Reflection

Answer these honestly to build smarter habits.

• Did I make an offer or invite someone to buy

Yes ☐ No ☐

• Did anyone ask about my product, price, or service

Yes ☐ No ☐

• Did I earn income this week

Yes ☐ No ☐

If yes, write how much:

Income earned: _____

If no, write what you will do differently:

Adjustment next week: _____

Time and Effort Check

How consistent were you this week

☐ I worked each day I planned

☐ I worked on fewer days than planned

☐ I did not follow my plan but learned something useful

Total time spent: _____ hours or minutes

What to Improve

Reflect on one small change that could make next week better. Improvement means simplifying, not adding more work.

One change I will make next week:

Next Week Action Boost

Choose one habit to repeat for better results next week.

☐ Share customer feedback

☐ Promote my offer once per day

☐ Reach out to potential customers

☐ Track time and income daily

☐ Improve my product or service

Chapter 11
Week 5: Build

This page helps you begin each week with clarity. Your goal is to focus on the few actions that move your side hustle forward. Write short, specific answers that you can act on daily.

This Week's Focus

What is the single most important result you want by the end of this week?

My weekly focus:

This Week's Top Three Goals

Choose three goals that directly support your focus. These must be outcomes, not tasks.

1

2

3

Before choosing tasks, make sure each goal leads to progress you can measure or deliver.

Key Action Steps

Break each goal into actions you can complete this week. Keep them clear and simple.

• Goal 1 action steps:

• Goal 2 action steps:

• Goal 3 action steps:

Customer Connection Plan

How will you connect with people who need your offer this week

Think messages, research, sharing value, asking questions, or inviting interest.

Plan to connect:

Time Commitment

How much time will you dedicate this week

Choose a realistic schedule you can promise yourself.

I will commit:

☐ 10 to 30 minutes daily

☐ 45 to 60 minutes daily

☐ Certain days only: _____

Success Reminder

Write a short sentence that describes success for this week. Keep it inspiring and specific.

Success for me this week means:

Weekly Action Plan Checklist

You may use this checklist throughout your side hustle journey, these actions create real progress whether you are choosing your idea, building your offer, or selling it. Mark off tasks as you complete them and aim for consistency, not perfection.

1. Build or Improve the Offer

Your product or service becomes stronger when you work on it a little at a time.

☐ I worked on something customers will receive

☐ I improved one step or feature of my offer

☐ I simplified or removed something that was not needed

☐ I prepared a version that can be delivered faster or easier

> Progress means improving what exists, not adding more work.

2. Connect With Real People

Talking to people helps you understand what they need and how you can help.

☐ I asked questions to learn what people struggle with

☐ I started a conversation about a need or problem

☐ I listened to feedback or concerns

☐ I invited someone to learn more about my offer

> Connection is more valuable than followers or likes.

3. Promote With Purpose

Customers need reminders, clarity, and visibility. Promotion helps them see how you can help.

☐ I shared what problem I solve

☐ I explained the result my offer delivers

☐ I told people how to buy or book

☐ I posted, messaged, or shared something helpful and relevant

People cannot buy what they cannot see clearly.

4. Track Time and Money

Tracking creates honest awareness. Awareness creates smarter decisions.

☐ I tracked time spent on my business

☐ I tracked expenses or materials used

☐ I recorded income or potential leads

☐ I noted where effort produced the best results

Better tracking leads to better pricing and better profit.

5. Learn One Thing that Makes You Better

Growth does not require long study sessions. One useful insight each week is enough.

☐ I learned from customer feedback

☐ I studied a question or topic related to my niche

☐ I observed what competitors are doing well

☐ I practiced a skill that helps my delivery or promotion

Mini insight of the week:

Learning is only useful when combined with action.

Weekly Completion Check

☐ I completed the actions that matter most

☐ I moved closer to income through simple steps

☐ I worked consistently rather than trying to be perfect

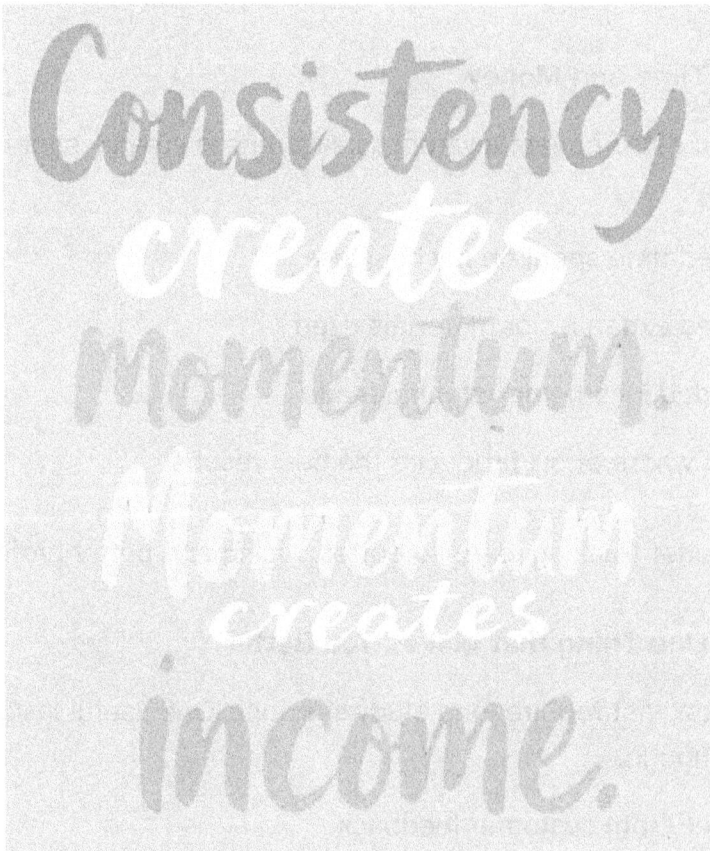

.

Mini Learning Prompt

Each week, take a few minutes to learn something that makes your business stronger. The goal is not to study endlessly. The goal is to gain one insight that helps you sell, deliver, or improve your offer. Use this page to focus your learning and turn knowledge into action.

This Week's Question

Choose one question that helps you understand your market, your offer, or your customer. You can write your own or pick from the list below.

My learning question of the week:

Ideas for Learning Questions

Pick one if you need inspiration.

- What result do people want most from my offer
- What frustrates customers about current solutions
- What small improvement would make my offer more valuable
- What type of content or message gets the most attention
- What do customers complain about in my niche
- What topics do people ask questions about again and again

- How do others in my niche describe the problem I solve

- What skill could I improve that would increase my value

- What do successful sellers do that I can learn from

- How could I deliver my product or service faster or more clearly

What I Discovered

Write your insight in one to three sentences. Keep it clear and practical.

My learning insight:

How I Will Use This Insight

Learning matters only when it leads to action. Choose a small step you can take based on what you learned.

One change or improvement I will make:?

_____

Every week you learn something useful, you become more valuable. More value creates more income.

Weekly Budget and Cost Tracker

Strong businesses manage money from the start. This page helps you track what you spend and what you earn during the week. You are learning how to make profit without high costs or guesswork.

Weekly Budget Plan

Plan your spending before the week starts. Keep it lean and practical. Only spend money that supports profit or delivery.

Planned spending this week:

What will I invest in and why

(example: materials, tools, ads, packaging)

Spend for value, not for excitement. Simple solutions often cost less and work better.

Cost Breakdown

List any expenses that support your side hustle. Include business tools, supplies, shipping, packaging, digital tools, ads, or delivery costs.

Date

Expense Item

Purpose

Cost

Total spent this week: _____

· · ·

Income Received

List any income earned from products, services, or pre orders.

Date

Customer or Order

Product or Service

Amount

Total income this week: _____

Profit and Results

Calculate your weekly outcome.

Profit or loss this week

Income minus expenses: _____

How this week helped my business

Reflect on what worked financially.

☐ I kept costs low

☐ I improved how I price

☐ I created value without overspending

☐ I learned what customers respond to

☐ I focused on smart investments

Savings and Future Planning

If you saved money this week, note how you will use it in the future.

Savings or remaining budget: _____

Next week financial adjustment:_____

Smart spending
builds
profit

Profit grows

your business steadely

Weekly Marketing Task

Choose one strategic marketing action this week. The goal is to share your offer with clarity and intention so people know how you can help them. Pick a single task and complete it before the week ends.

This Week's Marketing Task

Write one clear promotional action. Keep it specific.

My task:

Who Is This For

Identify the type of person this message or action is meant to reach.

Target audience:

What Value Will I Share

Explain the benefit, result, or helpful insight you will communicate.

Value or benefit:

Where Will I Share It

Choose the place or method. Examples include a post, story, message, email, conversation, group, or platform.

☐ Social post

☐ Direct message

☐ Community group

☐ Short video

☐ Email

☐ In person

☐ Other: _____

What Is the Call to Action

Tell people what to do next. Example: message you, ask a question, buy, book, request more info.

Call to action:

Follow Up and Results

After completing the task, fill in your results.

How many people engaged or responded

What questions did people ask

What worked well about this message

What I will try or repeat next week

●————————●

Marketing works through clarity and repetition, not pressure. Real questions, real value, and real conversations lead to sales.

Weekly Review and Sales Reflection

At the end of each week, pause and check what you learned, what you earned, and what you can improve. This reflection helps you build a stronger offer without working harder. Focus on real progress, not perfection.

Weekly Wins

List anything that worked well, big or small. Wins include effort, actions, conversations, clarity, and sales.

This week

I am proud of:

Customer Insight

People teach you what they value. Write any feedback, questions, compliments, problems, or requests you heard this week.

Feedback or insights from real people:

Sales Reflection

Answer these honestly to build smarter habits.

• Did I make an offer or invite someone to buy

Yes ☐ No ☐

• Did anyone ask about my product, price, or service

Yes ☐ No ☐

• Did I earn income this week

Yes ☐ No ☐

If yes, write how much:

Income earned: _____

If no, write what you will do differently:

Adjustment next week: _____

Time and Effort Check

How consistent were you this week

☐ I worked each day I planned

☐ I worked on fewer days than planned

☐ I did not follow my plan but learned something useful

Total time spent: _____ hours or minutes

What to Improve

Reflect on one small change that could make next week better. Improvement means simplifying, not adding more work.

One change I will make next week:

Next Week Action Boost

Choose one habit to repeat for better results next week.

☐ Share customer feedback

☐ Promote my offer once per day

☐ Reach out to potential customers

☐ Track time and income daily

☐ Improve my product or service

Chapter 12
Week 6: Prepare

This page helps you begin each week with clarity. Your goal is to focus on the few actions that move your side hustle forward. Write short, specific answers that you can act on daily.

This Week's Focus

What is the single most important result you want by the end of this week?

My weekly focus:

This Week's Top Three Goals

Choose three goals that directly support your focus. These must be outcomes, not tasks.

1

2

3

Before choosing tasks, make sure each goal leads to progress you can measure or deliver.

Key Action Steps

Break each goal into actions you can complete this week. Keep them clear and simple.

• Goal 1 action steps:

• Goal 2 action steps:

• Goal 3 action steps:

Customer Connection Plan

How will you connect with people who need your offer this week

Think messages, research, sharing value, asking questions, or inviting interest.

Plan to connect:

Time Commitment

How much time will you dedicate this week

Choose a realistic schedule you can promise yourself.

I will commit:

☐ 10 to 30 minutes daily

☐ 45 to 60 minutes daily

☐ Certain days only: _____

Success Reminder

Write a short sentence that describes success for this week. Keep it inspiring and specific.

Success for me this week means:

Weekly Action Plan Checklist

You may use this checklist throughout your side hustle journey, these actions create real progress whether you are choosing your idea, building your offer, or selling it. Mark off tasks as you complete them and aim for consistency, not perfection.

1. Build or Improve the Offer

Your product or service becomes stronger when you work on it a little at a time.

☐ I worked on something customers will receive

☐ I improved one step or feature of my offer

☐ I simplified or removed something that was not needed

☐ I prepared a version that can be delivered faster or easier

> Progress means improving what exists, not adding more work.

2. Connect With Real People

Talking to people helps you understand what they need and how you can help.

☐ I asked questions to learn what people struggle with

☐ I started a conversation about a need or problem

☐ I listened to feedback or concerns

☐ I invited someone to learn more about my offer

> Connection is more valuable than followers or likes.

3. Promote With Purpose

Customers need reminders, clarity, and visibility. Promotion helps them see how you can help.

☐ I shared what problem I solve

☐ I explained the result my offer delivers

☐ I told people how to buy or book

☐ I posted, messaged, or shared something helpful and relevant

People cannot buy what they cannot see clearly.

4. Track Time and Money

Tracking creates honest awareness. Awareness creates smarter decisions.

☐ I tracked time spent on my business

☐ I tracked expenses or materials used

☐ I recorded income or potential leads

☐ I noted where effort produced the best results

Better tracking leads to better pricing and better profit.

5. Learn One Thing that Makes You Better

Growth does not require long study sessions. One useful insight each week is enough.

☐ I learned from customer feedback

☐ I studied a question or topic related to my niche

☐ I observed what competitors are doing well

☐ I practiced a skill that helps my delivery or promotion

Mini insight of the week:

Learning is only useful when combined with action.

Weekly Completion Check

☐ I completed the actions that matter most

☐ I moved closer to income through simple steps

☐ I worked consistently rather than trying to be perfect

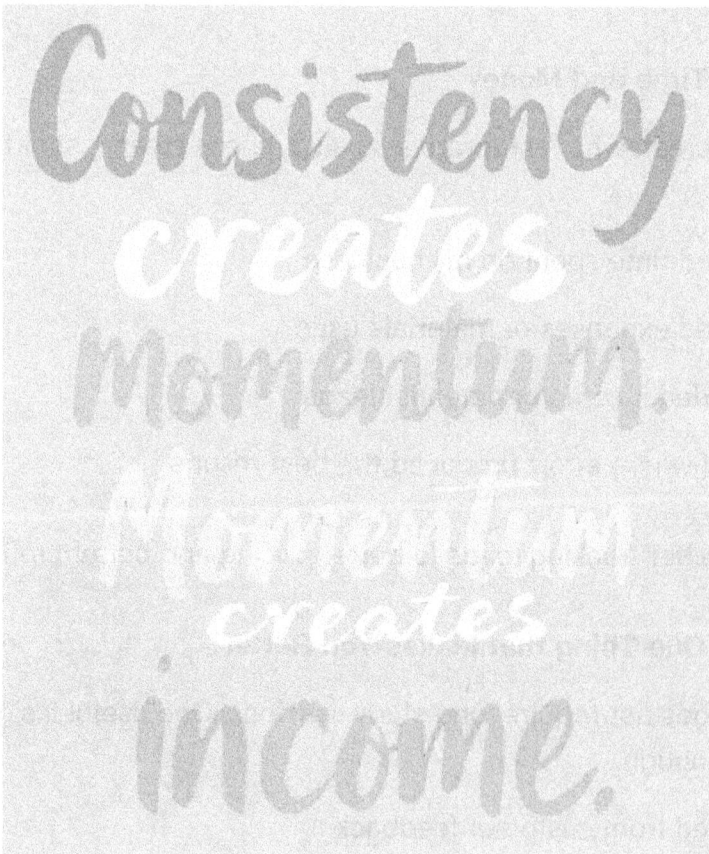

Consistency creates momentum. Momentum creates income.

Mini Learning Prompt

Each week, take a few minutes to learn something that makes your business stronger. The goal is not to study endlessly. The goal is to gain one insight that helps you sell, deliver, or improve your offer. Use this page to focus your learning and turn knowledge into action.

This Week's Question

Choose one question that helps you understand your market, your offer, or your customer. You can write your own or pick from the list below.

My learning question of the week:

Ideas for Learning Questions

Pick one if you need inspiration.

- What result do people want most from my offer

- What frustrates customers about current solutions

- What small improvement would make my offer more valuable

- What type of content or message gets the most attention

- What do customers complain about in my niche

- What topics do people ask questions about again and again

- How do others in my niche describe the problem I solve

- What skill could I improve that would increase my value

- What do successful sellers do that I can learn from

- How could I deliver my product or service faster or more clearly

What I Discovered

Write your insight in one to three sentences. Keep it clear and practical.

My learning insight:

How I Will Use This Insight

Learning matters only when it leads to action. Choose a small step you can take based on what you learned.

One change or improvement I will make:?

_____

Every week you learn something useful, you become more valuable. More value creates more income.

Weekly Budget and Cost Tracker

Strong businesses manage money from the start. This page helps you track what you spend and what you earn during the week. You are learning how to make profit without high costs or guesswork.

Weekly Budget Plan

Plan your spending before the week starts. Keep it lean and practical. Only spend money that supports profit or delivery.

Planned spending this week:

What will I invest in and why

(example: materials, tools, ads, packaging)

Spend for value, not for excitement. Simple solutions often cost less and work better.

Cost Breakdown

List any expenses that support your side hustle. Include business tools, supplies, shipping, packaging, digital tools, ads, or delivery costs.

Date

Expense Item

Purpose

Cost

Total spent this week: _____

. . .

Income Received

List any income earned from products, services, or pre orders.

Date

Customer or Order

Product or Service

Amount

Total income this week: _____

Profit and Results

Calculate your weekly outcome.

Profit or loss this week

Income minus expenses: _____

How this week helped my business

Reflect on what worked financially.

☐ I kept costs low

☐ I improved how I price

☐ I created value without overspending

☐ I learned what customers respond to

☐ I focused on smart investments

Savings and Future Planning

If you saved money this week, note how you will use it in the future.

Savings or remaining budget: _____

**Next week financial
adjustment:**_____

Smart spending
builds
profit
Profit grows
your business steadely

Weekly Marketing Task

Choose one strategic marketing action this week. The goal is to share your offer with clarity and intention so people know how you can help them. Pick a single task and complete it before the week ends.

This Week's Marketing Task

Write one clear promotional action. Keep it specific.

My task:

Who Is This For

Identify the type of person this message or action is meant to reach.

Target audience:

What Value Will I Share

Explain the benefit, result, or helpful insight you will communicate.

Value or benefit:

Where Will I Share It

Choose the place or method. Examples include a post, story, message, email, conversation, group, or platform.

☐ Social post

☐ Direct message

☐ Community group

☐ Short video

☐ Email

☐ In person

☐ Other: _____

What Is the Call to Action

Tell people what to do next. Example: message you, ask a question, buy, book, request more info.

Call to action:

Follow Up and Results

After completing the task, fill in your results.

How many people engaged or responded

What questions did people ask

What worked well about this message

What I will try or repeat next week

● —————————— ●

Marketing works through clarity and repetition, not pressure. Real questions, real value, and real conversations lead to sales.

Weekly Review and Sales Reflection

At the end of each week, pause and check what you learned, what you earned, and what you can improve. This reflection helps you build a stronger offer without working harder. Focus on real progress, not perfection.

Weekly Wins

List anything that worked well, big or small. Wins include effort, actions, conversations, clarity, and sales.

This week

I am proud of:

Customer Insight

People teach you what they value. Write any feedback, questions, compliments, problems, or requests you heard this week.

Feedback or insights from real people:

Sales Reflection

Answer these honestly to build smarter habits.

• Did I make an offer or invite someone to buy

Yes ☐ No ☐

• Did anyone ask about my product, price, or service

Yes ☐ No ☐

• Did I earn income this week

Yes ☐ No ☐

If yes, write how much:

Income earned: _____

If no, write what you will do differently:

Adjustment next week: _____

Time and Effort Check

How consistent were you this week

☐ I worked each day I planned

☐ I worked on fewer days than planned

☐ I did not follow my plan but learned something useful

Total time spent: _____ hours or minutes

What to Improve

Reflect on one small change that could make next week better. Improvement means simplifying, not adding more work.

One change I will make next week:

Next Week Action Boost

Choose one habit to repeat for better results next week.

☐ Share customer feedback

☐ Promote my offer once per day

☐ Reach out to potential customers

☐ Track time and income daily

☐ Improve my product or service

Chapter 13
Week 7: Launch

This page helps you begin each week with clarity. Your goal is to focus on the few actions that move your side hustle forward. Write short, specific answers that you can act on daily.

This Week's Focus

What is the single most important result you want by the end of this week?

My weekly focus:

This Week's Top Three Goals

Choose three goals that directly support your focus. These must be outcomes, not tasks.

1

2

3

Before choosing tasks, make sure each goal leads to progress you can measure or deliver.

Key Action Steps

Break each goal into actions you can complete this week. Keep them clear and simple.

• Goal 1 action steps:

• Goal 2 action steps:

• Goal 3 action steps:

Customer Connection Plan

How will you connect with people who need your offer this week

Think messages, research, sharing value, asking questions, or inviting interest.

Plan to connect:

Time Commitment

How much time will you dedicate this week

Choose a realistic schedule you can promise yourself.

I will commit:

☐ 10 to 30 minutes daily

☐ 45 to 60 minutes daily

☐ Certain days only: _____

Success Reminder

Write a short sentence that describes success for this week. Keep it inspiring and specific.

Success for me this week means:

Weekly Action Plan Checklist

You may use this checklist throughout your side hustle journey, these actions create real progress whether you are choosing your idea, building your offer, or selling it. Mark off tasks as you complete them and aim for consistency, not perfection.

1. Build or Improve the Offer

Your product or service becomes stronger when you work on it a little at a time.

☐ I worked on something customers will receive

☐ I improved one step or feature of my offer

☐ I simplified or removed something that was not needed

☐ I prepared a version that can be delivered faster or easier

> Progress means improving what exists, not adding more work.

2. Connect With Real People

Talking to people helps you understand what they need and how you can help.

☐ I asked questions to learn what people struggle with

☐ I started a conversation about a need or problem

☐ I listened to feedback or concerns

☐ I invited someone to learn more about my offer

> Connection is more valuable than followers or likes.

3. Promote With Purpose

Customers need reminders, clarity, and visibility. Promotion helps them see how you can help.

☐ I shared what problem I solve

☐ I explained the result my offer delivers

☐ I told people how to buy or book

☐ I posted, messaged, or shared something helpful and relevant

People cannot buy what they cannot see clearly.

4. Track Time and Money

Tracking creates honest awareness. Awareness creates smarter decisions.

☐ I tracked time spent on my business

☐ I tracked expenses or materials used

☐ I recorded income or potential leads

☐ I noted where effort produced the best results

Better tracking leads to better pricing and better profit.

5. Learn One Thing that Makes You Better

Growth does not require long study sessions. One useful insight each week is enough.

☐ I learned from customer feedback

☐ I studied a question or topic related to my niche

☐ I observed what competitors are doing well

☐ I practiced a skill that helps my delivery or promotion

Mini insight of the week:

Learning is only useful when combined with action.

Weekly Completion Check

☐ I completed the actions that matter most

☐ I moved closer to income through simple steps

☐ I worked consistently rather than trying to be perfect

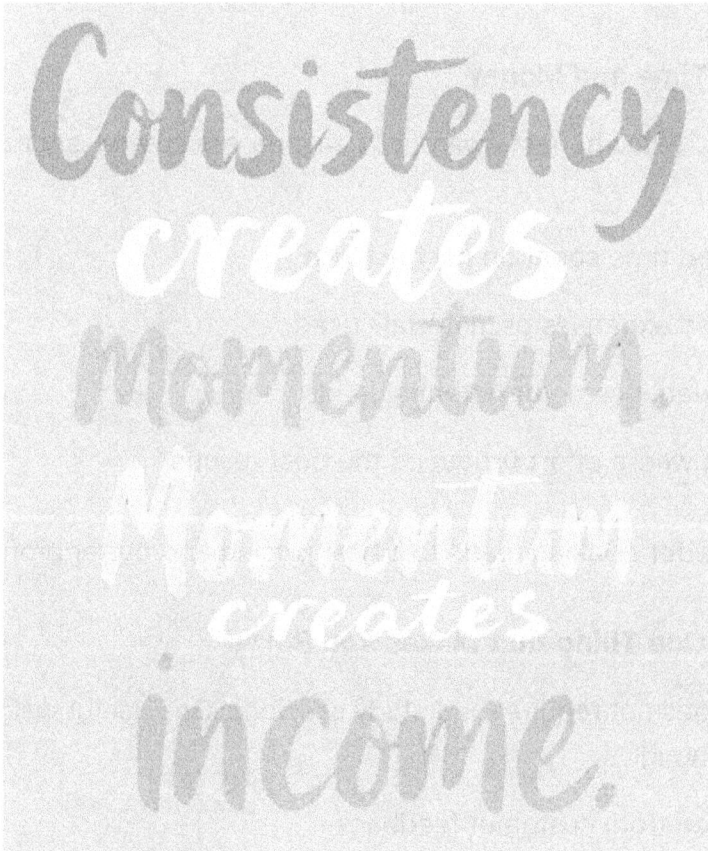

Mini Learning Prompt

Each week, take a few minutes to learn something that makes your business stronger. The goal is not to study endlessly. The goal is to gain one insight that helps you sell, deliver, or improve your offer. Use this page to focus your learning and turn knowledge into action.

This Week's Question

Choose one question that helps you understand your market, your offer, or your customer. You can write your own or pick from the list below.

My learning question of the week:

Ideas for Learning Questions

Pick one if you need inspiration.

• What result do people want most from my offer

• What frustrates customers about current solutions

• What small improvement would make my offer more valuable

• What type of content or message gets the most attention

• What do customers complain about in my niche

• What topics do people ask questions about again and again

- How do others in my niche describe the problem I solve

- What skill could I improve that would increase my value

- What do successful sellers do that I can learn from

- How could I deliver my product or service faster or more clearly

What I Discovered

Write your insight in one to three sentences. Keep it clear and practical.

My learning insight:

How I Will Use This Insight

Learning matters only when it leads to action. Choose a small step you can take based on what you learned.

One change or improvement I will make:?

_____

Every week you learn something useful, you become more valuable. More value creates more income.

Weekly Budget and Cost Tracker

Strong businesses manage money from the start. This page helps you track what you spend and what you earn during the week. You are learning how to make profit without high costs or guesswork.

Weekly Budget Plan

Plan your spending before the week starts. Keep it lean and practical. Only spend money that supports profit or delivery.

Planned spending this week:

What will I invest in and why

(example: materials, tools, ads, packaging)

Spend for value, not for excitement. Simple solutions often cost less and work better.

Cost Breakdown

List any expenses that support your side hustle. Include business tools, supplies, shipping, packaging, digital tools, ads, or delivery costs.

Date

Expense Item

Purpose

Cost

Total spent this week: _____

· · ·

Income Received

List any income earned from products, services, or pre orders.

Date

Customer or Order

Product or Service

Amount

Total income this week: _____

Profit and Results

Calculate your weekly outcome.

Profit or loss this week

Income minus expenses: _____

How this week helped my business

Reflect on what worked financially.

☐ I kept costs low

☐ I improved how I price

☐ I created value without overspending

☐ I learned what customers respond to

☐ I focused on smart investments

Savings and Future Planning

If you saved money this week, note how you will use it in the future.

Savings or remaining budget: _____

**Next week financial
adjustment:_____**

Smart spending
builds
profit
Profit grows
your business steadely

Weekly Marketing Task

Choose one strategic marketing action this week. The goal is to share your offer with clarity and intention so people know how you can help them. Pick a single task and complete it before the week ends.

This Week's Marketing Task

Write one clear promotional action. Keep it specific.

My task:

Who Is This For

Identify the type of person this message or action is meant to reach.

Target audience:

What Value Will I Share

Explain the benefit, result, or helpful insight you will communicate.

Value or benefit:

Where Will I Share It

Choose the place or method. Examples include a post, story, message, email, conversation, group, or platform.

☐ Social post

☐ Direct message

☐ Community group

☐ Short video

☐ Email

☐ In person

☐ Other: _____

What Is the Call to Action

Tell people what to do next. Example: message you, ask a question, buy, book, request more info.

Call to action:

Follow Up and Results

After completing the task, fill in your results.

How many people engaged or responded

What questions did people ask

What worked well about this message

What I will try or repeat next week

●————————————●

Marketing works through clarity and repetition, not pressure. Real questions, real value, and real conversations lead to sales.

Weekly Review and Sales Reflection

At the end of each week, pause and check what you learned, what you earned, and what you can improve. This reflection helps you build a stronger offer without working harder. Focus on real progress, not perfection.

Weekly Wins

List anything that worked well, big or small. Wins include effort, actions, conversations, clarity, and sales.

This week

I am proud of:

Customer Insight

People teach you what they value. Write any feedback, questions, compliments, problems, or requests you heard this week.

Feedback or insights from real people:

Sales Reflection

Answer these honestly to build smarter habits.

• Did I make an offer or invite someone to buy

Yes ☐ No ☐

• Did anyone ask about my product, price, or service

Yes ☐ No ☐

• Did I earn income this week

Yes ☐ No ☐

If yes, write how much:

Income earned: _____

If no, write what you will do differently:

Adjustment next week: _____

Time and Effort Check

How consistent were you this week

☐ I worked each day I planned

☐ I worked on fewer days than planned

☐ I did not follow my plan but learned something useful

Total time spent: _____ hours or minutes

What to Improve

Reflect on one small change that could make next week better. Improvement means simplifying, not adding more work.

One change I will make next week:

Next Week Action Boost

Choose one habit to repeat for better results next week.

☐ Share customer feedback

☐ Promote my offer once per day

☐ Reach out to potential customers

☐ Track time and income daily

☐ Improve my product or service

Chapter 14
Week 8: Learn

This page helps you begin each week with clarity. Your goal is to focus on the few actions that move your side hustle forward. Write short, specific answers that you can act on daily.

This Week's Focus

What is the single most important result you want by the end of this week?

My weekly focus:

This Week's Top Three Goals

Choose three goals that directly support your focus. These must be outcomes, not tasks.

1

2

3

Before choosing tasks, make sure each goal leads to progress you can measure or deliver.

Key Action Steps

Break each goal into actions you can complete this week. Keep them clear and simple.

• Goal 1 action steps:

• Goal 2 action steps:

• Goal 3 action steps:

Customer Connection Plan

How will you connect with people who need your offer this week

Think messages, research, sharing value, asking questions, or inviting interest.

Plan to connect:

Time Commitment

How much time will you dedicate this week

Choose a realistic schedule you can promise yourself.

I will commit:

☐ 10 to 30 minutes daily

☐ 45 to 60 minutes daily

☐ Certain days only: _____

Success Reminder

Write a short sentence that describes success for this week. Keep it inspiring and specific.

Success for me this week means:

Evan West

Weekly Action Plan Checklist

You may use this checklist throughout your side hustle journey, these actions create real progress whether you are choosing your idea, building your offer, or selling it. Mark off tasks as you complete them and aim for consistency, not perfection.

1. Build or Improve the Offer

Your product or service becomes stronger when you work on it a little at a time.

☐ I worked on something customers will receive

☐ I improved one step or feature of my offer

☐ I simplified or removed something that was not needed

☐ I prepared a version that can be delivered faster or easier

> Progress means improving what exists, not adding more work.

2. Connect With Real People

Talking to people helps you understand what they need and how you can help.

☐ I asked questions to learn what people struggle with

☐ I started a conversation about a need or problem

☐ I listened to feedback or concerns

☐ I invited someone to learn more about my offer

> Connection is more valuable than followers or likes.

3. Promote With Purpose

Customers need reminders, clarity, and visibility. Promotion helps them see how you can help.

☐ I shared what problem I solve

☐ I explained the result my offer delivers

☐ I told people how to buy or book

☐ I posted, messaged, or shared something helpful and relevant

People cannot buy what they cannot see clearly.

4. Track Time and Money

Tracking creates honest awareness. Awareness creates smarter decisions.

☐ I tracked time spent on my business

☐ I tracked expenses or materials used

☐ I recorded income or potential leads

☐ I noted where effort produced the best results

Better tracking leads to better pricing and better profit.

5. Learn One Thing that Makes You Better

Growth does not require long study sessions. One useful insight each week is enough.

☐ I learned from customer feedback

☐ I studied a question or topic related to my niche

☐ I observed what competitors are doing well

☐ I practiced a skill that helps my delivery or promotion

Mini insight of the week:

Learning is only useful when combined with action.

Weekly Completion Check

☐ I completed the actions that matter most

☐ I moved closer to income through simple steps

☐ I worked consistently rather than trying to be perfect

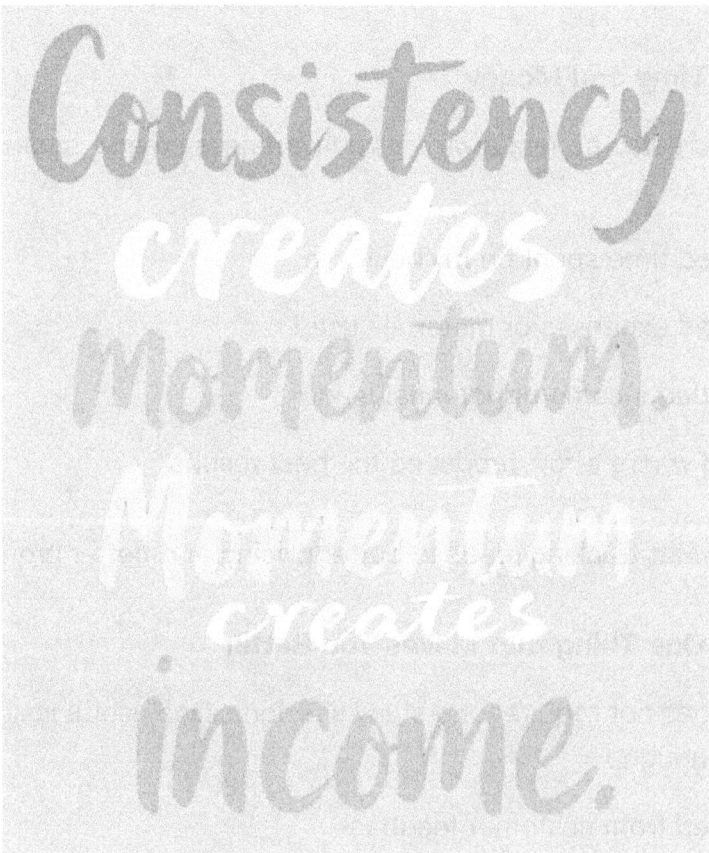

Mini Learning Prompt

Each week, take a few minutes to learn something that makes your business stronger. The goal is not to study endlessly. The goal is to gain one insight that helps you sell, deliver, or improve your offer. Use this page to focus your learning and turn knowledge into action.

This Week's Question

Choose one question that helps you understand your market, your offer, or your customer. You can write your own or pick from the list below.

My learning question of the week:

Ideas for Learning Questions

Pick one if you need inspiration.

- What result do people want most from my offer

- What frustrates customers about current solutions

- What small improvement would make my offer more valuable

- What type of content or message gets the most attention

- What do customers complain about in my niche

- What topics do people ask questions about again and again

- How do others in my niche describe the problem I solve

- What skill could I improve that would increase my value

- What do successful sellers do that I can learn from

- How could I deliver my product or service faster or more clearly

What I Discovered

Write your insight in one to three sentences. Keep it clear and practical.

My learning insight:

How I Will Use This Insight

Learning matters only when it leads to action. Choose a small step you can take based on what you learned.

One change or improvement I will make:?

Every week you learn something useful, you become more valuable. More value creates more income.

Weekly Budget and Cost Tracker

Strong businesses manage money from the start. This page helps you track what you spend and what you earn during the week. You are learning how to make profit without high costs or guesswork.

Weekly Budget Plan

Plan your spending before the week starts. Keep it lean and practical. Only spend money that supports profit or delivery.

Planned spending this week:

What will I invest in and why

(example: materials, tools, ads, packaging)

Spend for value, not for excitement. Simple solutions often cost less and work better.

Cost Breakdown

List any expenses that support your side hustle. Include business tools, supplies, shipping, packaging, digital tools, ads, or delivery costs.

Date

Expense Item

Purpose

Cost

Total spent this week: _____

· · ·

Income Received

List any income earned from products, services, or pre orders.

Date

Customer or Order

Product or Service

Amount

Total income this week: _____

Profit and Results

Calculate your weekly outcome.

Profit or loss this week

Income minus expenses: _____

How this week helped my business

Reflect on what worked financially.

☐ I kept costs low

☐ I improved how I price

☐ I created value without overspending

☐ I learned what customers respond to

☐ I focused on smart investments

Savings and Future Planning

If you saved money this week, note how you will use it in the future.

Savings or remaining budget: _____

**Next week financial
adjustment:_____**

Smart spending
builds
profit
Profit grows
your business steadely

Weekly Marketing Task

Choose one strategic marketing action this week. The goal is to share your offer with clarity and intention so people know how you can help them. Pick a single task and complete it before the week ends.

This Week's Marketing Task

Write one clear promotional action. Keep it specific.

My task:

Who Is This For

Identify the type of person this message or action is meant to reach.

Target audience:

What Value Will I Share

Explain the benefit, result, or helpful insight you will communicate.

Value or benefit:

Where Will I Share It

Choose the place or method. Examples include a post, story, message, email, conversation, group, or platform.

☐ Social post

☐ Direct message

☐ Community group

☐ Short video

☐ Email

☐ In person

☐ Other: _____

What Is the Call to Action

Tell people what to do next. Example: message you, ask a question, buy, book, request more info.

Call to action:

Follow Up and Results

After completing the task, fill in your results.

How many people engaged or responded

What questions did people ask

What worked well about this message

What I will try or repeat next week

●————————●

Marketing works through clarity and repetition, not pressure. Real questions, real value, and real conversations lead to sales.

Weekly Review and Sales Reflection

At the end of each week, pause and check what you learned, what you earned, and what you can improve. This reflection helps you build a stronger offer without working harder. Focus on real progress, not perfection.

Weekly Wins

List anything that worked well, big or small. Wins include effort, actions, conversations, clarity, and sales.

This week

I am proud of:

Customer Insight

People teach you what they value. Write any feedback, questions, compliments, problems, or requests you heard this week.

Feedback or insights from real people:

Sales Reflection

Answer these honestly to build smarter habits.

• Did I make an offer or invite someone to buy

Yes ☐ No ☐

• Did anyone ask about my product, price, or service

Yes ☐ No ☐

• Did I earn income this week

Yes ☐ No ☐

If yes, write how much:

Income earned: _____

If no, write what you will do differently:

Adjustment next week: _____

Time and Effort Check

How consistent were you this week

☐ I worked each day I planned

☐ I worked on fewer days than planned

☐ I did not follow my plan but learned something useful

Total time spent: _____ hours or minutes

What to Improve

Reflect on one small change that could make next week better. Improvement means simplifying, not adding more work.

One change I will make next week:

Next Week Action Boost

Choose one habit to repeat for better results next week.

☐ Share customer feedback

☐ Promote my offer once per day

☐ Reach out to potential customers

☐ Track time and income daily

☐ Improve my product or service

Chapter 15
Week 9: Improve

This page helps you begin each week with clarity. Your goal is to focus on the few actions that move your side hustle forward. Write short, specific answers that you can act on daily.

This Week's Focus

What is the single most important result you want by the end of this week?

My weekly focus:

This Week's Top Three Goals

Choose three goals that directly support your focus. These must be outcomes, not tasks.

1

2

3

Before choosing tasks, make sure each goal leads to progress you can measure or deliver.

Key Action Steps

Break each goal into actions you can complete this week. Keep them clear and simple.

- Goal 1 action steps:

- Goal 2 action steps:

- Goal 3 action steps:

Customer Connection Plan

How will you connect with people who need your offer this week

Think messages, research, sharing value, asking questions, or inviting interest.

Plan to connect:

Time Commitment

How much time will you dedicate this week

Choose a realistic schedule you can promise yourself.

I will commit:

☐ 10 to 30 minutes daily

☐ 45 to 60 minutes daily

☐ Certain days only: _____

Success Reminder

Write a short sentence that describes success for this week. Keep it inspiring and specific.

Success for me this week means:

Weekly Action Plan Checklist

You may use this checklist throughout your side hustle journey, these actions create real progress whether you are choosing your idea, building your offer, or selling it. Mark off tasks as you complete them and aim for consistency, not perfection.

1. Build or Improve the Offer

Your product or service becomes stronger when you work on it a little at a time.

☐ I worked on something customers will receive

☐ I improved one step or feature of my offer

☐ I simplified or removed something that was not needed

☐ I prepared a version that can be delivered faster or easier

> Progress means improving what exists, not adding more work.

2. Connect With Real People

Talking to people helps you understand what they need and how you can help.

☐ I asked questions to learn what people struggle with

☐ I started a conversation about a need or problem

☐ I listened to feedback or concerns

☐ I invited someone to learn more about my offer

> Connection is more valuable than followers or likes.

3. Promote With Purpose

Customers need reminders, clarity, and visibility. Promotion helps them see how you can help.

☐ I shared what problem I solve

☐ I explained the result my offer delivers

☐ I told people how to buy or book

☐ I posted, messaged, or shared something helpful and relevant

People cannot buy what they cannot see clearly.

4. Track Time and Money

Tracking creates honest awareness. Awareness creates smarter decisions.

☐ I tracked time spent on my business

☐ I tracked expenses or materials used

☐ I recorded income or potential leads

☐ I noted where effort produced the best results

Better tracking leads to better pricing and better profit.

5. Learn One Thing that Makes You Better

Growth does not require long study sessions. One useful insight each week is enough.

☐ I learned from customer feedback

☐ I studied a question or topic related to my niche

☐ I observed what competitors are doing well

☐ I practiced a skill that helps my delivery or promotion

Mini insight of the week:

Learning is only useful when combined with action.

Weekly Completion Check

☐ I completed the actions that matter most

☐ I moved closer to income through simple steps

☐ I worked consistently rather than trying to be perfect

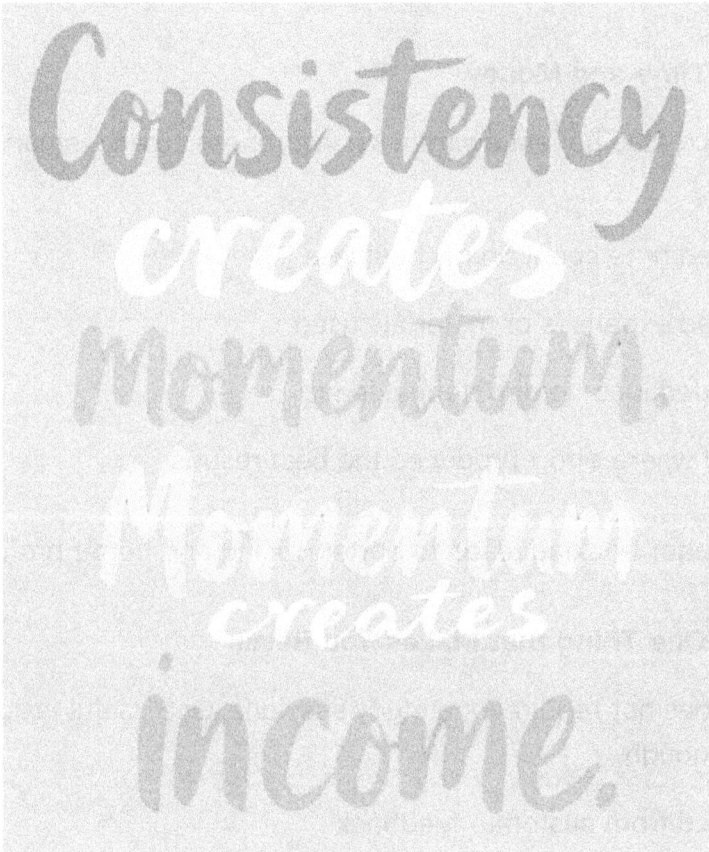

.

Mini Learning Prompt

Each week, take a few minutes to learn something that makes your business stronger. The goal is not to study endlessly. The goal is to gain one insight that helps you sell, deliver, or improve your offer. Use this page to focus your learning and turn knowledge into action.

This Week's Question

Choose one question that helps you understand your market, your offer, or your customer. You can write your own or pick from the list below.

My learning question of the week:

Ideas for Learning Questions

Pick one if you need inspiration.

- What result do people want most from my offer

- What frustrates customers about current solutions

- What small improvement would make my offer more valuable

- What type of content or message gets the most attention

- What do customers complain about in my niche

- What topics do people ask questions about again and again

- How do others in my niche describe the problem I solve

- What skill could I improve that would increase my value

- What do successful sellers do that I can learn from

- How could I deliver my product or service faster or more clearly

What I Discovered

Write your insight in one to three sentences. Keep it clear and practical.

My learning insight:

How I Will Use This Insight

Learning matters only when it leads to action. Choose a small step you can take based on what you learned.

One change or improvement I will make:?

_____

Every week you learn something useful, you become more valuable. More value creates more income.

Weekly Budget and Cost Tracker

Strong businesses manage money from the start. This page helps you track what you spend and what you earn during the week. You are learning how to make profit without high costs or guesswork.

Weekly Budget Plan

Plan your spending before the week starts. Keep it lean and practical. Only spend money that supports profit or delivery.

Planned spending this week:

What will I invest in and why

(example: materials, tools, ads, packaging)

Spend for value, not for excitement. Simple solutions often cost less and work better.

Cost Breakdown

List any expenses that support your side hustle. Include business tools, supplies, shipping, packaging, digital tools, ads, or delivery costs.

Date

Expense Item

Purpose

Cost

Total spent this week: _____

· · ·

Income Received

List any income earned from products, services, or pre orders.

Date

Customer or Order

Product or Service

Amount

Total income this week: _____

Profit and Results

Calculate your weekly outcome.

Profit or loss this week

Income minus expenses: _____

How this week helped my business

Reflect on what worked financially.

☐ I kept costs low

☐ I improved how I price

☐ I created value without overspending

☐ I learned what customers respond to

☐ I focused on smart investments

Savings and Future Planning

If you saved money this week, note how you will use it in the future.

Savings or remaining budget: _____

**Next week financial
adjustment:**_____

Smart spending builds profit

Profit grows
your business steadely

Weekly Marketing Task

Choose one strategic marketing action this week. The goal is to share your offer with clarity and intention so people know how you can help them. Pick a single task and complete it before the week ends.

This Week's Marketing Task

Write one clear promotional action. Keep it specific.

My task:

Who Is This For

Identify the type of person this message or action is meant to reach.

Target audience:

What Value Will I Share

Explain the benefit, result, or helpful insight you will communicate.

Value or benefit:

Where Will I Share It

Choose the place or method. Examples include a post, story, message, email, conversation, group, or platform.

☐ Social post

☐ Direct message

☐ Community group

☐ Short video

☐ Email

☐ In person

☐ Other: _____

What Is the Call to Action

Tell people what to do next. Example: message you, ask a question, buy, book, request more info.

Call to action:

Follow Up and Results

After completing the task, fill in your results.

How many people engaged or responded

What questions did people ask

What worked well about this message

What I will try or repeat next week

● ———————————— ●

Marketing works through clarity and repetition, not pressure. Real questions, real value, and real conversations lead to sales.

Weekly Review and Sales Reflection

At the end of each week, pause and check what you learned, what you earned, and what you can improve. This reflection helps you build a stronger offer without working harder. Focus on real progress, not perfection.

Weekly Wins

List anything that worked well, big or small. Wins include effort, actions, conversations, clarity, and sales.

This week

I am proud of:

Customer Insight

People teach you what they value. Write any feedback, questions, compliments, problems, or requests you heard this week.

Feedback or insights from real people:

Sales Reflection

Answer these honestly to build smarter habits.

• Did I make an offer or invite someone to buy

Yes ☐ No ☐

• Did anyone ask about my product, price, or service

Yes ☐ No ☐

• Did I earn income this week

Yes ☐ No ☐

If yes, write how much:

Income earned: _____

If no, write what you will do differently:

Adjustment next week: _____

Time and Effort Check

How consistent were you this week

☐ I worked each day I planned

☐ I worked on fewer days than planned

☐ I did not follow my plan but learned something useful

Total time spent: _____ hours or minutes

What to Improve

Reflect on one small change that could make next week better. Improvement means simplifying, not adding more work.

One change I will make next week:

Next Week Action Boost

Choose one habit to repeat for better results next week.

☐ Share customer feedback

☐ Promote my offer once per day

☐ Reach out to potential customers

☐ Track time and income daily

☐ Improve my product or service

Chapter 16
Week 10: Promote

This page helps you begin each week with clarity. Your goal is to focus on the few actions that move your side hustle forward. Write short, specific answers that you can act on daily.

This Week's Focus

What is the single most important result you want by the end of this week?

My weekly focus:

This Week's Top Three Goals

Choose three goals that directly support your focus. These must be outcomes, not tasks.

1

2

3

Before choosing tasks, make sure each goal leads to progress you can measure or deliver.

Key Action Steps

Break each goal into actions you can complete this week. Keep them clear and simple.

• Goal 1 action steps:

• Goal 2 action steps:

• Goal 3 action steps:

Customer Connection Plan

How will you connect with people who need your offer this week

Think messages, research, sharing value, asking questions, or inviting interest.

Plan to connect:

Time Commitment

How much time will you dedicate this week

Choose a realistic schedule you can promise yourself.

I will commit:

☐ 10 to 30 minutes daily

☐ 45 to 60 minutes daily

☐ Certain days only: _____

Success Reminder

Write a short sentence that describes success for this week. Keep it inspiring and specific.

Success for me this week means:

Weekly Action Plan Checklist

You may use this checklist throughout your side hustle journey, these actions create real progress whether you are choosing your idea, building your offer, or selling it. Mark off tasks as you complete them and aim for consistency, not perfection.

1. Build or Improve the Offer

Your product or service becomes stronger when you work on it a little at a time.

☐ I worked on something customers will receive

☐ I improved one step or feature of my offer

☐ I simplified or removed something that was not needed

☐ I prepared a version that can be delivered faster or easier

> Progress means improving what exists, not adding more work.

2. Connect With Real People

Talking to people helps you understand what they need and how you can help.

☐ I asked questions to learn what people struggle with

☐ I started a conversation about a need or problem

☐ I listened to feedback or concerns

☐ I invited someone to learn more about my offer

> Connection is more valuable than followers or likes.

3. Promote With Purpose

Customers need reminders, clarity, and visibility. Promotion helps them see how you can help.

☐ I shared what problem I solve

☐ I explained the result my offer delivers

☐ I told people how to buy or book

☐ I posted, messaged, or shared something helpful and relevant

People cannot buy what they cannot see clearly.

4. Track Time and Money

Tracking creates honest awareness. Awareness creates smarter decisions.

☐ I tracked time spent on my business

☐ I tracked expenses or materials used

☐ I recorded income or potential leads

☐ I noted where effort produced the best results

Better tracking leads to better pricing and better profit.

5. Learn One Thing that Makes You Better

Growth does not require long study sessions. One useful insight each week is enough.

☐ I learned from customer feedback

☐ I studied a question or topic related to my niche

☐ I observed what competitors are doing well

☐ I practiced a skill that helps my delivery or promotion

Mini insight of the week:

Learning is only useful when combined with action.

Weekly Completion Check

☐ I completed the actions that matter most

☐ I moved closer to income through simple steps

☐ I worked consistently rather than trying to be perfect

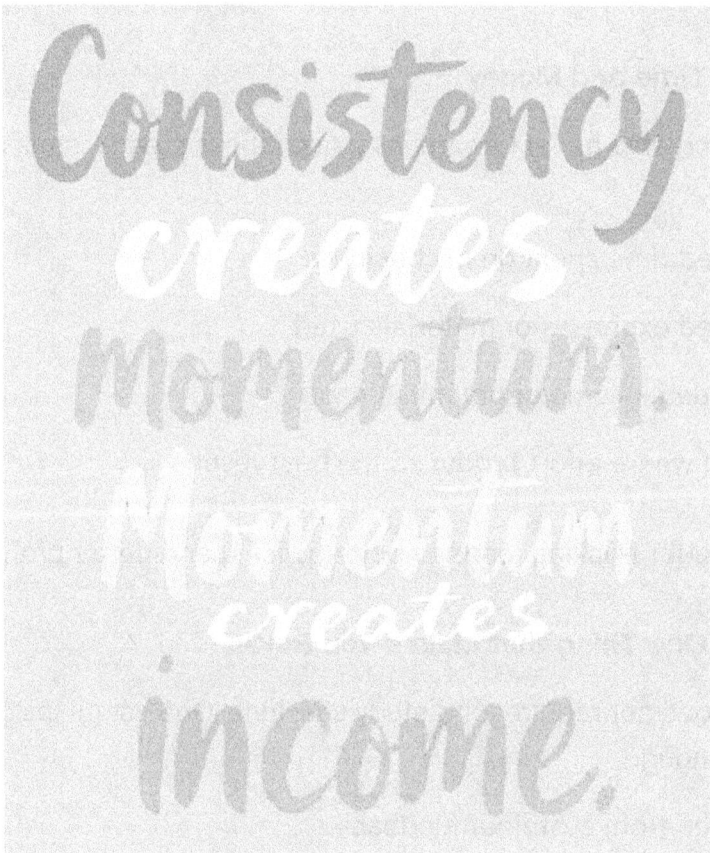

Consistency creates momentum. Momentum creates income.

.

Mini Learning Prompt

Each week, take a few minutes to learn something that makes your business stronger. The goal is not to study endlessly. The goal is to gain one insight that helps you sell, deliver, or improve your offer. Use this page to focus your learning and turn knowledge into action.

This Week's Question

Choose one question that helps you understand your market, your offer, or your customer. You can write your own or pick from the list below.

My learning question of the week:

Ideas for Learning Questions

Pick one if you need inspiration.

- What result do people want most from my offer

- What frustrates customers about current solutions

- What small improvement would make my offer more valuable

- What type of content or message gets the most attention

- What do customers complain about in my niche

- What topics do people ask questions about again and again

- How do others in my niche describe the problem I solve

- What skill could I improve that would increase my value

- What do successful sellers do that I can learn from

- How could I deliver my product or service faster or more clearly

What I Discovered

Write your insight in one to three sentences. Keep it clear and practical.

My learning insight:

How I Will Use This Insight

Learning matters only when it leads to action. Choose a small step you can take based on what you learned.

One change or improvement I will make:?

_____

Every week you learn something useful, you become more valuable. More value creates more income.

Weekly Budget and Cost Tracker

Strong businesses manage money from the start. This page helps you track what you spend and what you earn during the week. You are learning how to make profit without high costs or guesswork.

Weekly Budget Plan

Plan your spending before the week starts. Keep it lean and practical. Only spend money that supports profit or delivery.

Planned spending this week:

What will I invest in and why

(example: materials, tools, ads, packaging)

Spend for value, not for excitement. Simple solutions often cost less and work better.

Cost Breakdown

List any expenses that support your side hustle. Include business tools, supplies, shipping, packaging, digital tools, ads, or delivery costs.

Date

Expense Item

Purpose

Cost

Total spent this week: _____

· · ·

Income Received

List any income earned from products, services, or pre orders.

Date

Customer or Order

Product or Service

Amount

Total income this week: _____

Profit and Results

Calculate your weekly outcome.

Profit or loss this week

Income minus expenses: _____

How this week helped my business

Reflect on what worked financially.

☐ I kept costs low

☐ I improved how I price

☐ I created value without overspending

☐ I learned what customers respond to

☐ I focused on smart investments

Savings and Future Planning

If you saved money this week, note how you will use it in the future.

Savings or remaining budget: _____

Next week financial adjustment:_____

Smart spending
builds
profit
Profit grows
your business steadely

Weekly Marketing Task

Choose one strategic marketing action this week. The goal is to share your offer with clarity and intention so people know how you can help them. Pick a single task and complete it before the week ends.

This Week's Marketing Task

Write one clear promotional action. Keep it specific.

My task:

Who Is This For

Identify the type of person this message or action is meant to reach.

Target audience:

What Value Will I Share

Explain the benefit, result, or helpful insight you will communicate.

Value or benefit:

Where Will I Share It

Choose the place or method. Examples include a post, story, message, email, conversation, group, or platform.

☐ Social post

☐ Direct message

☐ Community group

☐ Short video

☐ Email

☐ In person

☐ Other: _____

What Is the Call to Action

Tell people what to do next. Example: message you, ask a question, buy, book, request more info.

Call to action:

Follow Up and Results

After completing the task, fill in your results.

How many people engaged or responded

What questions did people ask

What worked well about this message

What I will try or repeat next week

●────────●

Marketing works through clarity and repetition, not pressure. Real questions, real value, and real conversations lead to sales.

Weekly Review and Sales Reflection

At the end of each week, pause and check what you learned, what you earned, and what you can improve. This reflection helps you build a stronger offer without working harder. Focus on real progress, not perfection.

Weekly Wins

List anything that worked well, big or small. Wins include effort, actions, conversations, clarity, and sales.

This week

I am proud of:

Customer Insight

People teach you what they value. Write any feedback, questions, compliments, problems, or requests you heard this week.

Feedback or insights from real people:

Sales Reflection

Answer these honestly to build smarter habits.

• Did I make an offer or invite someone to buy

Yes ☐ No ☐

• Did anyone ask about my product, price, or service

Yes ☐ No ☐

• Did I earn income this week

Yes ☐ No ☐

If yes, write how much:

Income earned: _____

If no, write what you will do differently:

Adjustment next week: _____

Time and Effort Check

How consistent were you this week

☐ I worked each day I planned

☐ I worked on fewer days than planned

☐ I did not follow my plan but learned something useful

Total time spent: _____ hours or minutes

What to Improve

Reflect on one small change that could make next week better. Improvement means simplifying, not adding more work.

One change I will make next week:

Next Week Action Boost

Choose one habit to repeat for better results next week.

☐ Share customer feedback

☐ Promote my offer once per day

☐ Reach out to potential customers

☐ Track time and income daily

☐ Improve my product or service

Chapter 17
Week 11: Grow

This page helps you begin each week with clarity. Your goal is to focus on the few actions that move your side hustle forward. Write short, specific answers that you can act on daily.

This Week's Focus

What is the single most important result you want by the end of this week?

My weekly focus:

This Week's Top Three Goals

Choose three goals that directly support your focus. These must be outcomes, not tasks.

1

2

3

Before choosing tasks, make sure each goal leads to progress you can measure or deliver.

Key Action Steps

Break each goal into actions you can complete this week. Keep them clear and simple.

- Goal 1 action steps:

- Goal 2 action steps:

- Goal 3 action steps:

Customer Connection Plan

How will you connect with people who need your offer this week

Think messages, research, sharing value, asking questions, or inviting interest.

Plan to connect:

Time Commitment

How much time will you dedicate this week

Choose a realistic schedule you can promise yourself.

I will commit:

☐ 10 to 30 minutes daily

☐ 45 to 60 minutes daily

☐ Certain days only: _____

Success Reminder

Write a short sentence that describes success for this week. Keep it inspiring and specific.

Success for me this week means:

Weekly Action Plan Checklist

You may use this checklist throughout your side hustle journey, these actions create real progress whether you are choosing your idea, building your offer, or selling it. Mark off tasks as you complete them and aim for consistency, not perfection.

1. Build or Improve the Offer

Your product or service becomes stronger when you work on it a little at a time.

☐ I worked on something customers will receive

☐ I improved one step or feature of my offer

☐ I simplified or removed something that was not needed

☐ I prepared a version that can be delivered faster or easier

> Progress means improving what exists, not adding more work.

2. Connect With Real People

Talking to people helps you understand what they need and how you can help.

☐ I asked questions to learn what people struggle with

☐ I started a conversation about a need or problem

☐ I listened to feedback or concerns

☐ I invited someone to learn more about my offer

> Connection is more valuable than followers or likes.

3. Promote With Purpose

Customers need reminders, clarity, and visibility. Promotion helps them see how you can help.

☐ I shared what problem I solve

☐ I explained the result my offer delivers

☐ I told people how to buy or book

☐ I posted, messaged, or shared something helpful and relevant

People cannot buy what they cannot see clearly.

4. Track Time and Money

Tracking creates honest awareness. Awareness creates smarter decisions.

☐ I tracked time spent on my business

☐ I tracked expenses or materials used

☐ I recorded income or potential leads

☐ I noted where effort produced the best results

Better tracking leads to better pricing and better profit.

5. Learn One Thing that Makes You Better

Growth does not require long study sessions. One useful insight each week is enough.

☐ I learned from customer feedback

☐ I studied a question or topic related to my niche

☐ I observed what competitors are doing well

☐ I practiced a skill that helps my delivery or promotion

Mini insight of the week:

Learning is only useful when combined with action.

Weekly Completion Check

☐ I completed the actions that matter most

☐ I moved closer to income through simple steps

☐ I worked consistently rather than trying to be perfect

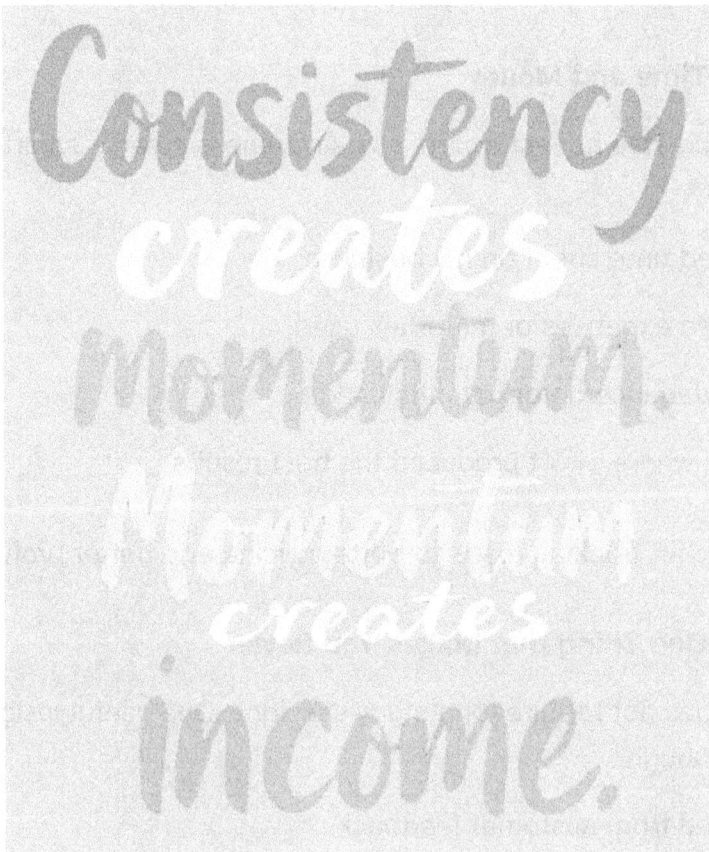

.

Mini Learning Prompt

Each week, take a few minutes to learn something that makes your business stronger. The goal is not to study endlessly. The goal is to gain one insight that helps you sell, deliver, or improve your offer. Use this page to focus your learning and turn knowledge into action.

This Week's Question

Choose one question that helps you understand your market, your offer, or your customer. You can write your own or pick from the list below.

My learning question of the week:

Ideas for Learning Questions

Pick one if you need inspiration.

- What result do people want most from my offer

- What frustrates customers about current solutions

- What small improvement would make my offer more valuable

- What type of content or message gets the most attention

- What do customers complain about in my niche

- What topics do people ask questions about again and again

- How do others in my niche describe the problem I solve

- What skill could I improve that would increase my value

- What do successful sellers do that I can learn from

- How could I deliver my product or service faster or more clearly

What I Discovered

Write your insight in one to three sentences. Keep it clear and practical.

My learning insight:

How I Will Use This Insight

Learning matters only when it leads to action. Choose a small step you can take based on what you learned.

One change or improvement I will make:?

_____

Every week you learn something useful, you become more valuable. More value creates more income.

Weekly Budget and Cost Tracker

Strong businesses manage money from the start. This page helps you track what you spend and what you earn during the week. You are learning how to make profit without high costs or guesswork.

Weekly Budget Plan

Plan your spending before the week starts. Keep it lean and practical. Only spend money that supports profit or delivery.

Planned spending this week:

What will I invest in and why

(example: materials, tools, ads, packaging)

Spend for value, not for excitement. Simple solutions often cost less and work better.

Cost Breakdown

List any expenses that support your side hustle. Include business tools, supplies, shipping, packaging, digital tools, ads, or delivery costs.

Date

Expense Item

Purpose

Cost

Total spent this week: _____

. . .

Income Received

List any income earned from products, services, or pre orders.

Date

Customer or Order

Product or Service

Amount

Total income this week: _____

Profit and Results

Calculate your weekly outcome.

Profit or loss this week

Income minus expenses: _____

How this week helped my business

Reflect on what worked financially.

☐ I kept costs low

☐ I improved how I price

☐ I created value without overspending

☐ I learned what customers respond to

☐ I focused on smart investments

Savings and Future Planning

If you saved money this week, note how you will use it in the future.

Savings or remaining budget: _____

Next week financial adjustment:_____

Smart spending
builds
profit
Profit grows
your business steadely

Weekly Marketing Task

Choose one strategic marketing action this week. The goal is to share your offer with clarity and intention so people know how you can help them. Pick a single task and complete it before the week ends.

This Week's Marketing Task

Write one clear promotional action. Keep it specific.

My task:

Who Is This For

Identify the type of person this message or action is meant to reach.

Target audience:

What Value Will I Share

Explain the benefit, result, or helpful insight you will communicate.

Value or benefit:

Where Will I Share It

Choose the place or method. Examples include a post, story, message, email, conversation, group, or platform.

☐ Social post

☐ Direct message

☐ Community group

☐ Short video

☐ Email

☐ In person

☐ Other: _____

What Is the Call to Action

Tell people what to do next. Example: message you, ask a question, buy, book, request more info.

Call to action:

Follow Up and Results

After completing the task, fill in your results.

How many people engaged or responded

What questions did people ask

What worked well about this message

What I will try or repeat next week

●————————●

Marketing works through clarity and repetition, not pressure. Real questions, real value, and real conversations lead to sales.

Weekly Review and Sales Reflection

At the end of each week, pause and check what you learned, what you earned, and what you can improve. This reflection helps you build a stronger offer without working harder. Focus on real progress, not perfection.

Weekly Wins

List anything that worked well, big or small. Wins include effort, actions, conversations, clarity, and sales.

This week

I am proud of:

Customer Insight

People teach you what they value. Write any feedback, questions, compliments, problems, or requests you heard this week.

Feedback or insights from real people:

Sales Reflection

Answer these honestly to build smarter habits.

• Did I make an offer or invite someone to buy

Yes ☐ No ☐

• Did anyone ask about my product, price, or service

Yes ☐ No ☐

• Did I earn income this week

Yes ☐ No ☐

If yes, write how much:

Income earned: _____

If no, write what you will do differently:

Adjustment next week: _____

Time and Effort Check

How consistent were you this week

☐ I worked each day I planned

☐ I worked on fewer days than planned

☐ I did not follow my plan but learned something useful

Total time spent: _____ hours or minutes

What to Improve

Reflect on one small change that could make next week better. Improvement means simplifying, not adding more work.

One change I will make next week:

Next Week Action Boost

Choose one habit to repeat for better results next week.

☐ Share customer feedback

☐ Promote my offer once per day

☐ Reach out to potential customers

☐ Track time and income daily

☐ Improve my product or service

Chapter 18
Week 12: Celebrate

This page helps you begin each week with clarity. Your goal is to focus on the few actions that move your side hustle forward. Write short, specific answers that you can act on daily.

This Week's Focus

What is the single most important result you want by the end of this week?

My weekly focus:

This Week's Top Three Goals

Choose three goals that directly support your focus. These must be outcomes, not tasks.

1

2

3

Before choosing tasks, make sure each goal leads to progress you can measure or deliver.

Key Action Steps

Break each goal into actions you can complete this week. Keep them clear and simple.

• Goal 1 action steps:

• Goal 2 action steps:

• Goal 3 action steps:

Customer Connection Plan

How will you connect with people who need your offer this week

Think messages, research, sharing value, asking questions, or inviting interest.

Plan to connect:

Time Commitment

How much time will you dedicate this week

Choose a realistic schedule you can promise yourself.

I will commit:

☐ 10 to 30 minutes daily

☐ 45 to 60 minutes daily

☐ Certain days only: _____

Success Reminder

Write a short sentence that describes success for this week. Keep it inspiring and specific.

Success for me this week means:

Weekly Action Plan Checklist

You may use this checklist throughout your side hustle journey, these actions create real progress whether you are choosing your idea, building your offer, or selling it. Mark off tasks as you complete them and aim for consistency, not perfection.

1. Build or Improve the Offer

Your product or service becomes stronger when you work on it a little at a time.

☐ I worked on something customers will receive

☐ I improved one step or feature of my offer

☐ I simplified or removed something that was not needed

☐ I prepared a version that can be delivered faster or easier

> Progress means improving what exists, not adding more work.

2. Connect With Real People

Talking to people helps you understand what they need and how you can help.

☐ I asked questions to learn what people struggle with

☐ I started a conversation about a need or problem

☐ I listened to feedback or concerns

☐ I invited someone to learn more about my offer

> Connection is more valuable than followers or likes.

3. Promote With Purpose

Customers need reminders, clarity, and visibility. Promotion helps them see how you can help.

☐ I shared what problem I solve

☐ I explained the result my offer delivers

☐ I told people how to buy or book

☐ I posted, messaged, or shared something helpful and relevant

People cannot buy what they cannot see clearly.

4. Track Time and Money

Tracking creates honest awareness. Awareness creates smarter decisions.

☐ I tracked time spent on my business

☐ I tracked expenses or materials used

☐ I recorded income or potential leads

☐ I noted where effort produced the best results

Better tracking leads to better pricing and better profit.

5. Learn One Thing that Makes You Better

Growth does not require long study sessions. One useful insight each week is enough.

☐ I learned from customer feedback

☐ I studied a question or topic related to my niche

☐ I observed what competitors are doing well

☐ I practiced a skill that helps my delivery or promotion

Mini insight of the week:

Learning is only useful when combined with action.

Weekly Completion Check

☐ I completed the actions that matter most

☐ I moved closer to income through simple steps

☐ I worked consistently rather than trying to be perfect

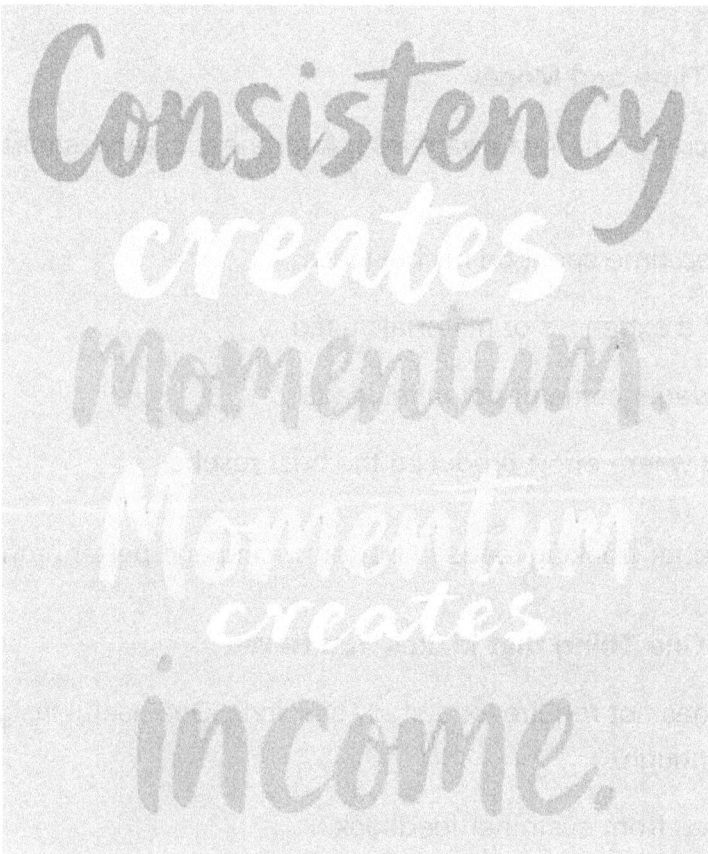

Consistency creates momentum. Momentum creates income.

Mini Learning Prompt

Each week, take a few minutes to learn something that makes your business stronger. The goal is not to study endlessly. The goal is to gain one insight that helps you sell, deliver, or improve your offer. Use this page to focus your learning and turn knowledge into action.

This Week's Question

Choose one question that helps you understand your market, your offer, or your customer. You can write your own or pick from the list below.

My learning question of the week:

Ideas for Learning Questions

Pick one if you need inspiration.

• What result do people want most from my offer

• What frustrates customers about current solutions

• What small improvement would make my offer more valuable

• What type of content or message gets the most attention

• What do customers complain about in my niche

• What topics do people ask questions about again and again

- How do others in my niche describe the problem I solve

- What skill could I improve that would increase my value

- What do successful sellers do that I can learn from

- How could I deliver my product or service faster or more clearly

What I Discovered

Write your insight in one to three sentences. Keep it clear and practical.

My learning insight:

How I Will Use This Insight

Learning matters only when it leads to action. Choose a small step you can take based on what you learned.

One change or improvement I will make:?

_____

Every week you learn something useful, you become more valuable. More value creates more income.

Weekly Budget and Cost Tracker

Strong businesses manage money from the start. This page helps you track what you spend and what you earn during the week. You are learning how to make profit without high costs or guesswork.

Weekly Budget Plan

Plan your spending before the week starts. Keep it lean and practical. Only spend money that supports profit or delivery.

Planned spending this week:

What will I invest in and why

(example: materials, tools, ads, packaging)

Spend for value, not for excitement. Simple solutions often cost less and work better.

Cost Breakdown

List any expenses that support your side hustle. Include business tools, supplies, shipping, packaging, digital tools, ads, or delivery costs.

Date

Expense Item

Purpose

Cost

Total spent this week: _____

. . .

Income Received

List any income earned from products, services, or pre orders.

Date

Customer or Order

Product or Service

Amount

Total income this week: _____

Profit and Results

Calculate your weekly outcome.

Profit or loss this week

Income minus expenses: _____

How this week helped my business

Reflect on what worked financially.

☐ I kept costs low

☐ I improved how I price

☐ I created value without overspending

☐ I learned what customers respond to

☐ I focused on smart investments

Savings and Future Planning

If you saved money this week, note how you will use it in the future.

Savings or remaining budget: _____

Next week financial adjustment:_____

Smart spending

builds

profit

Profit grows

your business steadely

Weekly Marketing Task

Choose one strategic marketing action this week. The goal is to share your offer with clarity and intention so people know how you can help them. Pick a single task and complete it before the week ends.

This Week's Marketing Task

Write one clear promotional action. Keep it specific.

My task:

Who Is This For

Identify the type of person this message or action is meant to reach.

Target audience:

What Value Will I Share

Explain the benefit, result, or helpful insight you will communicate.

Value or benefit:

Where Will I Share It

Choose the place or method. Examples include a post, story, message, email, conversation, group, or platform.

☐ Social post

☐ Direct message

☐ Community group

☐ Short video

☐ Email

☐ In person

☐ Other: _____

What Is the Call to Action

Tell people what to do next. Example: message you, ask a question, buy, book, request more info.

Call to action:

Follow Up and Results

After completing the task, fill in your results.

How many people engaged or responded

What questions did people ask

What worked well about this message

What I will try or repeat next week

●——————————●

Marketing works through clarity and repetition, not pressure. Real questions, real value, and real conversations lead to sales.

Weekly Review and Sales Reflection

At the end of each week, pause and check what you learned, what you earned, and what you can improve. This reflection helps you build a stronger offer without working harder. Focus on real progress, not perfection.

Weekly Wins

List anything that worked well, big or small. Wins include effort, actions, conversations, clarity, and sales.

This week

I am proud of:

Customer Insight

People teach you what they value. Write any feedback, questions, compliments, problems, or requests you heard this week.

Feedback or insights from real people:

Sales Reflection

Answer these honestly to build smarter habits.

• Did I make an offer or invite someone to buy

Yes ☐ No ☐

• Did anyone ask about my product, price, or service

Yes ☐ No ☐

• Did I earn income this week

Yes ☐ No ☐

If yes, write how much:

Income earned: _____

If no, write what you will do differently:

Adjustment next week: _____

Time and Effort Check

How consistent were you this week

☐ I worked each day I planned

☐ I worked on fewer days than planned

☐ I did not follow my plan but learned something useful

Total time spent: _____ hours or minutes

What to Improve

Reflect on one small change that could make next week better. Improvement means simplifying, not adding more work.

One change I will make next week:

Next Week Action Boost

Choose one habit to repeat for better results next week.

☐ Share customer feedback

☐ Promote my offer once per day

☐ Reach out to potential customers

☐ Track time and income daily

☐ Improve my product or service

Part 3

3 Monthly Checkpoints

Chapter 19
Month 1 Checkpoint: Validate and Learn

This month was about choosing and confirming a profitable idea. Your priority now is to compare expectations against results and extract actionable insight from what you learned.

Reality vs Goal Assessment

Evaluate what you planned versus what happened.

Goal

Planned Result

Actual Result

Gap Size

Small ☐ Medium ☐ Large ☐

Wins and Lessons

Write discoveries based on real conversations, interest, and feedback.

Wins:

Lessons:

Customer Insight

Record feedback and real reactions from potential buyers.

Customer Insight

Action to Take

Pivot or Persist

Based on results, choose your direction.

☐ Persist with the current offer

☐ Persist but refine the offer

☐ Pivot target audience

☐ Pivot product or service

☐ Pause to adjust delivery or pricing

Reason for this decision:

Pricing Adjustment

Decide whether pricing aligns with value.

☐ Keep current price

☐ Raise price

☐ Create a smaller starter version

☐ Create a premium version

Updated pricing or version:

Income and Expenses Summary

Track the financial outcome of Month 1.

Income

Source

Amount

Expenses

Item

Cost

Totals

- Total Income: _____

- Total Expenses: _____

- Profit or Loss: _____

Chapter 20

Month 2 Checkpoint: Improve and Earn

This month focused on building your first deliverable and launching it. Now review what improved your sales potential and what needs refinement.

Reality vs Goal Assessment

Compare performance with expectations.

Goal

Planned Result

Actual Result

Gap Size

Small ☐ Medium ☐ Large ☐

Wins and Lessons

Identify results and improvement opportunities based on real experience.

Wins:

Lessons:

Customer Insight

Focus on feedback connected to delivery, pricing, and value.

Customer Insight

Action to Take

Pivot or Persist

Select how you will move forward.

☐ Persist and promote consistently

☐ Persist but improve delivery

☐ Pivot to a clearer offer or format

☐ Pivot target audience

☐ Adjust pricing or offer structure

Reason for this decision:

Pricing Adjustment

Review whether pricing matched effort, demand, and perceived value.

☐ Keep price as is

☐ Raise price

☐ Create a higher priced premium version

☐ Create a low cost entry version

Updated pricing or version:

Income and Expenses Summary

Track the financial outcome of Month 2.

Income

Source

Amount

Expenses

Item

Cost

Totals

- Total Income: _____

- Total Expenses: _____

- Profit or Loss: _____

Chapter 21
Month 3 Checkpoint: Grow and Decide

This month is focused on improvement, consistent selling, and preparing for your long term strategy. Decide how your side hustle will continue after the first ninety days.

Reality vs Goal Assessment

Compare sales, delivery, and visibility to expectations.

Goal

Planned Result

Actual Result

Gap Size

Small ☐ Medium ☐ Large ☐

Wins and Lessons

Record strategic wins and improvements that created results.

Wins:

Lessons:

Customer Insight

Determine what customers value most and how to maximize it.

Customer Insight

Action to Take

Pivot or Persist

Choose how your offer will continue to grow.

☐ Persist and scale gradually

☐ Persist with improved delivery

☐ Introduce a higher value premium version

☐ Launch a starter version to widen access

☐ Pivot to a more profitable audience

Reason for this decision:

Pricing Adjustment

Use real data to refine pricing strategy.

☐ Keep current price

☐ Increase price to match value

☐ Introduce tiered pricing

☐ Remove low profit options

Updated pricing or version:

Income and Expenses Summary

Assess Month 3 financial outcome.

Income

Source

Amount

Expenses

Item

Cost

Totals

- Total Income: _____

- Total Expenses: _____

- Profit or Loss: _____

Part 4
Your Momentum Toolkit

Chapter 22

14 Day Promotion Ideas

Simple actions to share
your offer with confidence

You worked hard to build something valuable. These small daily
promotion ideas help the world see it. Pick one each day or repeat
the ones that feel right. Confidence comes from showing up, not from
being perfect.

Day 1

Share one benefit or result of your offer

Day 2

Post a tip or helpful insight related to your niche

Day 3

Tell a short story about why you created your offer

Day 4

Share a behind the scenes look at how you deliver value

. . .

Day 5

Post a question that your ideal customer might ask

Day 6

Share one common mistake your offer helps people avoid

Day 7

Post a preview or demo of your product or service

Day 8

Share a quote, comment, or feedback you received

Day 9

Invite people to ask questions about your offer

Day 10

Share a small win or lesson you learned building your business

Day 11

Post a comparison: before and after using your offer

Day 12

Tell people who this offer is perfect for

Day 13

Explain the problem your offer solves in one clear sentence

Day 14

Share the price and invite the next buyer with confidence

> You do not need polished photos, perfect words, or a large audience. Show genuine effort. Share something real. People respond to honesty and clarity.

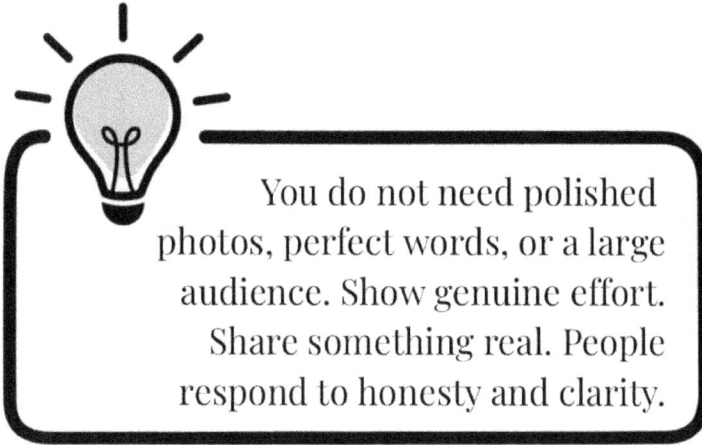

Celebrate visibility as progress. Every share counts as growth.

Chapter 23

Pricing and Profit Worksheet

Price with confidence
and protect your earnings

Your time, skill, and effort deserve fair compensation. Pricing is not just a number. It is a reflection of the value you create for someone who needs your help. This worksheet helps you choose a price that supports your income and respects your work.

Take a breath. You are allowed to earn well.

Step 1: List What You Deliver

Write the main outcome your customer receives and how it helps them.

What I deliver:

How it helps the customer:

Step 2: Estimate Time and Materials

Write the time and resources this offer requires.

Task or Material

Time or Cost

Total time spent: _____ hours or minutes

Total cost of materials: _____

Step 3: Calculate Your Minimum Income

Decide what your time is worth. This protects your profit.

My time value target (hourly): _____

Time cost estimate:

Time value target × time spent

= _____

Minimum price should cover:

Time + materials

= _____

Step 4: Check Market Value

A strong price reflects both effort and customer value. Answer these questions:

• Does this price match the result I am delivering

Yes ⊔ No ☐

• Do similar products or services cost more, equal, or less

More ☐ Equal ☐ Less ☐

• Would paying customers see this as high value

Yes ☐ No ☐

• Can I create a faster or premium version for a higher price

Yes ☐ No ☐

Step 5: Choose Your Price

Use the insights above to pick a price with confidence.

My selected price: _____

Optional versions:

• Starter version price: _____

• Premium version price: _____

REMINDER

You are not charging for the minutes you work.
You are charging for the outcome someone receives.

A fair price respects your effort and your customer's transformation.

Chapter 24

You are not charging for the minutes you work.

Know who you help
and why they need you

A successful offer does not need to help everyone. It only needs to help the right people. This mini sheet helps you understand who your ideal customer is, what they want, and how you can support them. The clearer you are, the easier it becomes to sell with confidence.

> You do not need a huge audience. You need a focused one.

Who I Help

Describe the kind of person who truly benefits from your offer.

This offer is for someone who:

Their Main Problem

Write the problem they are struggling with, in their words.

Their struggle or need:

Their Desired Result

People pay for outcomes. Describe what they want to achieve or feel.

They want to:

Their Emotional Motivation

Customers do not buy products. They buy feelings like ease, confidence, pride, or relief.

They want to feel:

☐ Confident

☐ Supported

☐ Proud

☐ Relieved

☐ Motivated

☐ Safe

☐ Other: _____

How My Offer Helps

Explain clearly how you help them reach their goal.

My offer helps them by:

REMEMBER! → The more clearly you understand who you help,the easier it becomes for them to see that you are the right choice.

Focus on helping one group well. Over time, more people will come.

Chapter 25

Side Hustle Tax Basics Tracker

Keep your records simple, clear, and stress free

A side hustle is a real business, and real businesses track income and expenses. You do not need complicated software to feel organized.

This tracker helps you keep basic records that make tax time easier. Think progress, not perfection.

You are building something worth tracking.

Income Log

Write any money earned from products, services, digital goods, events, or pre orders.

Date

Customer or Source

Product or Service

Amount

Total income logged: _____

Expense Log

Record costs related to your business. Many expenses can be tax deductible. Examples include supplies, shipping, tools, software, workspace materials, training, and promotional costs.

Date

Expense Item

Purpose

Cost

Total expenses logged: _____

Simple Tax Notes

Use this area to note questions, deductions to research, or categories to track more closely.

Notes:

REMINDER

You are not doing this alone. Every business owner learns as they go. Tracking your income and expenses is a sign of confidence, not perfection.

Keeping records is a way of honoring your effort. You deserve to earn clearly and proudly.

Chapter 26

Supplies and Tools Cost Estimator

Plan your resources
and protect your profit

Before you spend money on your business, take a moment to plan wisely. Tools and supplies should support your income, not drain it. This estimator helps you understand what you really need, what can wait, and what will create profit faster. You do not need everything at once. Start strong with what matters most.

Materials and Supplies

List physical items you need to deliver your product or service. Examples: packaging, ingredients, printing, art materials, inventory, samples.

Item

Purpose

One Time Cost

Ongoing Cost

Estimated total for materials: _____

. . .

Tools and Software

Include apps, subscriptions, equipment, or tools needed for creation or delivery. Examples: website tools, scheduling tools, editing apps, machines, digital platforms.

Tool or Software

Purpose

Cost

Monthly or One Time

Estimated total for tools: _____

Invest or Wait?

Mark which purchases support income right now, and which can wait until you grow more.

Smart investing means spending when it helps you earn, not just buying because it looks exciting.

Starter Budget

Choose a spending approach that fits your goals.

☐ Keep costs as low as possible

☐ Spend only on tools that increase profit

☐ Invest in quality because it reduces long term costs

☐ Mix and match: low cost now, upgrade later

My spending approach:

Every successful business started with something simple. What matters most is not how much you spend, but how consistently you create value.

Profit grows when you spend with intention. You are building a business, not buying one.

Chapter 27

Sales Tracking Graphs

Watch your progress and
celebrate growth you can see

Your sales tell a story. Every line, dot, and number shows effort
turning into results. These graphs help you track income month by
month so you can celebrate what is working and make confident
decisions about what comes next.

You are allowed to be
proud of growth at
every level.

Monthly Sales Progress Graph

Plot your income across the 3 months. Each point represents what
you earned. Connect them to see your journey clearly.

Instructions

• Mark your total income for each week

• Connect the points across the month

• Notice whether the line rises, holds steady, or needs attention

Week

Income

Week 1_____

Week 2_____

Week 3_____

Week 4_____

Graph Space Below

(Draw a line chart here in your book interior)

90 Day Sales Summary Graph

Track your income over the entire 90 days to see the bigger picture.

Instructions

• Mark your total income for each month

• Connect the dots to see overall growth

Month

Income

Month 1_____

Month 2_____

Month 3_____

Graph Space Below

. . .

Celebrating Progress

Answer one question after filling in each graph.

What helped your sales grow the most

-

-

-

-

-

What small change will help next month grow more

-

-

-

-

-

Growth does not always rise in a straight line. The important thing is that you are building, learning, and selling with intention.

**Every sale
represents trust.
Someone believed
in what you
created.
Celebrate that.**

Chapter 28

Final Review: Your Next 90 Days

Reflect, improve, and continue your growth

You built something real. You learned from customers, earned from your skills, and took consistent action. This review helps you build on that foundation by choosing what to continue, what to refine, and what to expand.

Growth is not about starting over. It is about building forward.

Your Wins

Write the achievements you are truly proud of. Include sales, feedback, progress, clarity, habits, or skills.

My biggest wins from this journey:

-

-

-

-

Your Valuable Lessons

Every challenge teaches something useful. Capture what will help you improve your business going forward.

Lessons I will carry into my next 90 days:

-

-

-

-

Customer Insights

Based on conversations, sales, feedback, and reactions, what do your customers value most about your offer

Insight

What I Will Do With It

Pivot or Scale

Choose your direction for the next 90 days. Be honest and strategic.

☐ **Scale what is working**

Keep your current offer and sell more consistently.

☐ **Refine and upgrade**

Improve delivery, results, or messaging to raise value.

☐ **Pivot offer or audience slightly**

Adjust to a clearer or more profitable need.

☐ **Expand with a new version**

Add a premium, starter, or digital option.

My path for the next 90 days:

Pricing Plan Forward

When you begin your next phase, how will your pricing support your business and your time

☐ Raise pricing to match value

☐ Keep pricing steady but improve delivery

☐ Create a premium version

☐ Add a lower cost starter

☐ Introduce tiered pricing

What I am choosing and why:

-

-

Income Target for the Next 90 Days

Write your confident income goal based on what you now know.

Next 90 day income target:

_____

How I will reach it:

☐ Consistent promotion

☐ Better delivery

☐ Improved messaging

☐ Higher value offer

☐ New offer version

☐ Customer retention

A Statement to Yourself

Complete this sentence with pride.

In my next 90 days, I will:

You are not starting from zero. You are building from experience. Your next 90 days grow from the strength of these first 90.

Afterword

You just committed ninety days to something bold and you chose to build something that did not exist before. That takes courage, patience, and belief in your own value - even if there were messy moments, slow weeks, and small doubts, you kept going - that matters more than anything else.

> **A side hustle is not only a business. It is a decision to trust your skills.**

It is proof that your time can create something meaningful. You learned from customers, made decisions based on real results, and earned with your own effort.

That is something to be proud of.

As you move forward, remember this: **success grows from consistency, not intensity.** You do not have to force rapid growth., and you do not have to compare yourself to larger businesses. You are building something unique, sustainable, built on your interests, your pace, and your goals.

There will always be more to learn, but now you know something powerful: **you can start anywhere and turn effort into income.** Not because everything is perfect, but because you showed up. You tested, improved, earned, corrected, refined, and tried again. That is what real success looks like.

Wherever you go from here, keep your curiosity, keep your courage, and keep your momentum.

You are no longer just thinking about ideas, you are building something people can trust, value, and pay for - you did it by honoring your time, your skills, and your growth.

Your effort is worth celebrating.

Here is to the next ninety days!